Leading Missional Change

Leading Missional Change

Move Your Congregation from Resistant to Re-Energized

PAUL J. DUNBAR
ANTHONY L. BLAIR

WIPF & STOCK · Eugene, Oregon

LEADING MISSIONAL CHANGE
Move Your Congregation from Resistant to Re-Energized

Copyright © 2013 Paul J. Dunbar and Anthony L. Blair. All rights reserved. Except for brief quotations in critical publications or reviews, no part of this book may be reproduced in any manner without prior written permission from the publisher. Write: Permissions, Wipf and Stock Publishers, 199 W. 8th Ave., Suite 3, Eugene, OR 97401.

Wipf & Stock
An Imprint of Wipf and Stock Publishers
199 W. 8th Ave., Suite 3
Eugene, OR 97401
www.wipfandstock.com

ISBN 13: 978-1-62032-789-0
Manufactured in the U.S.A.

All scripture quotations, unless otherwise indicated, are taken from the Holy Bible, New International Version®, NIV®. Copyright ©1973, 1978, 1984 by Biblica, Inc.™ Used by permission of Zondervan. All rights reserved worldwide.

*This book is dedicated affectionately to
the members of Bethany Evangelical Church.
Out of our deepest brokenness,
Jesus has brought us abundant blessings!*
—Paul

*I dedicate this to the good people of
Strinestown United Brethren Church,
who, together with our God,
redeemed my ministry
and taught me grace.*
—Tony

Contents

PART ONE: RESISTANCE

1 Keep the Change / 3
   When Churches Don't Want to Be on Mission

PART TWO: READINESS

2 Paul's Story / 19
   A Church That Wouldn't Change (But Did!)

3 Resistance Is Not Futile / 27
   Why Churches Don't Want to Be on Mission

4 Trust and Obey / 45
   How Churches Change to Be on Mission

5 Tony's Story / 67
   A Tale of Two Churches

6 A Little Research Project / 74
   Trust and Mission in Real Congregations

PART THREE: RE-ENERGIZING

7 Maintenance or Mission / 93
   One of These Churches May Be Yours

8 Your Mission, If You Choose to Accept It / 103
   Living Like a Follower of Jesus

Appendix A Congregational Trust Survey / 121
Appendix B Pastors' Follow-up Survey / 123
References and Resources / 125

PART ONE

Resistance

1

Keep the Change

When Churches Don't Want to Be on Mission

THREE VIGNETTES . . . AND WHY THERE IS A PROBLEM

FRANCES HAD AN AWAKENING when she moved from a rural setting to the city. She had been raised in a country village and had only served rural congregations, and now she found herself living and serving in a community that was struggling with all the usual urban social problems. There were drug deals on the corners and gunshots at night and some new form of vandalism every week. And it was heartbreaking to watch the kids in the neighborhood, many of them without loving parenting, many skipping school, their best chance to escape this life. Several decades before, this neighborhood had been the suburbs, but the city had grown out to it. The problem was that the congregation still considered itself a suburban church. Few actually lived in that neighborhood anymore, and most were rather blind to the challenges in the community around them when they worshipped together behind stain-glassed windows on Sunday morning. Pastor Frances was not blind . . . not anymore. Her heart bled for these people. So she proposed that the congregation create a youth center, to invite the kids off the streets and into the building to experience and hear the love of Jesus. It felt like a reasonable response of the people of God to spiritual and social needs right around them. The next thing Frances knew, her conference superintendent was scheduling a visit because he heard that there was dissension stirring in the congregation.

Tim was leading a congregation that had grown substantially in recent years. He had gradually come to recognize and be comfortable with his call to ministry and was now pleased with what God had done under his leadership. Yet he sensed that God was calling them into something more, that the church growth principles they had followed assiduously had brought in many warm bodies, but that most of his people were living at a rather shallow spiritual level. So he began to explore the heritage and literature of Christian spirituality, and discovered that through the centuries God's people had gone deeply into matters that he and others in his congregation were largely unaware of. Something opened up in Tim, and he plunged deeply into these studies. He found a new awakening in his soul. But when what he was learning found its way into his Sunday morning sermons, some congregation members balked. Others left, claiming that Tim had "gone Catholic" because some of the sources were pre-Reformation. The size of the congregation declined noticeably, with even some of those who stayed wishing out loud that Pastor Tim would just stick to preaching evangelistic sermons to seekers and save the deeper things for seminary.

Don was a traditional guy who served a traditional church, and he was rather okay with that. He felt no need to be flashy and he wasn't all that comfortable with technology. He did know how to love people, which is why he felt called to ministry to begin with. Pastoral care was his greatest passion. The folks in his congregation at First Church were mostly related to each other, and, despite the usual relational challenges, they took care of each other pretty well. It was a comfortable ministry for Don . . . except for his growing realization that the way they worshipped was increasingly disconnected from the culture of the community. Younger generations probably always complained that the older generations didn't want to change, but after nearly twenty years Don had seen one younger family after another leave their church, sometimes in sadness. So he proposed a radical solution to the worship team: that they start introducing some contemporary music into the service. He was astonished at the vehemence of the response, and at the reasons they gave for opposing this idea. He quickly dropped the idea, and First Church continued its slow decline into obsolescence.

These three vignettes and literally thousands of others like them illustrate a significant problem facing many American pastors and church leaders. Mission-minded leaders see the needs of people in their communities who do not yet know Christ and they explore new ways of reaching the unreached and discipling their own congregation members. However, in many cases, those members like their church and their faith just the way it is; it is comfortable for them and it seems to meet their needs today as well as it did years ago. Many resist any efforts to change, even if it means that new opportunities to evangelize the lost and to disciple new converts may be missed. Thus, those who find themselves called by God to do something transformative, those who can envision a greater good for their church or community, those who are motivated to change the status quo in the name of Jesus . . . these men and women often end up with cold water splashed in their faces when they attempt significant missional change in real congregations. Some push back and see their congregations divide. Some are fired or quit, and try again somewhere else. Some acquiesce and settle for the status quo. Some never recover.

These are sad stories, for, indeed, changes in American culture necessitate adaptations and transformations in congregational paradigms, attitudes, and structures in order that the mission Jesus gave the Church might be faithfully accomplished.[1] A genuine heart-level renewal of American believers and a recommitment to the mission Jesus gave are needed in order that each congregation might become what one has envisioned as "a community vibrant with life, pulsating with forgiveness, loud with celebration, fruitful in mission."[2] Ironically, one problem facing many congregations is that they were once missional . . . and the adaptations made in the past to speak with clarity to a previous generation ended up becoming new, deeply rooted traditions that impede further adaptation for later generations. And so congregations blindly or even passionately resist the replacement of those once-relevant traditions with missional change initiatives. Churches are social organizations and, as such, like any other organization or community they need to adapt continuously to changing cultural conditions, or they wither and die.[3] We have both visited churches where we had the distinct feeling of being in a time capsule. The churches were locked into a style of ministry that was effective in the mid-twentieth century, but the congregations were not speaking to the questions of the early twenty-first-century.

The purpose of this book is to give hope to leaders of such churches. In the pages that follow we explore the roots of congregational resistance to missional change and suggest ways to change a congregation's stance from

1. Rendle, *Leading Change*, 198.
2. McLaren, *Church on the Other Side*, 35.
3. Burke, "Even Healthy Churches Need to Change."

resistance to readiness for change and then even to re-energizing for mission. From our study of change initiatives in other contexts, we suggest that the key issue in overcoming resistance to change is relational and, more specifically, a matter of trust. Therefore, we examine the trust dynamics of pastoral leadership in a variety of contexts and propose some ways by which that trust can be translated into mission.

THE CHANGING FACE OF THE AMERICAN CHURCH

Continuous change is a fact of life in the early twenty-first century. Social scientists are recognizing that rapid and frequently chaotic changes are taking place in Western culture. Increasingly, people are recognizing that such changes are more than brief episodes after which people and organizations can stabilize and recover, and they are coming to a realization of the reality of "virtually continuous change."[4] Things have changed at a fundamental level and there is no going back. Continual change of this sort can be very disconcerting for organizations, especially churches, that prize stability and continuity. The pace of change in this world is increasing so rapidly, and churches, like other organizations, need to learn how to accelerate their "internal rate of change"[5] to keep pace. Churches may need to become more "organizationally agile,"[6] changing structures, paradigms and attitudes to connect with those who need Christ and to spiritually form those who already claim him. In our experience, there often has been a greater willingness on the part of congregants to resist such changes than there is to adapt to the changing needs of the surrounding cultures.

As the winds of change blow through twenty-first-century American churches and their surrounding communities, followers of Jesus are being called to complete the mission Jesus gave to his Church. Many church leaders are reexamining their beliefs about ecclesiology and even their own roles in this new environment. There is a growing abandonment of traditional ecclesiastical structures among some confessors of Christ and an increasing experimentation with new forms of worship and ministry. Many followers of Jesus are building bridges into the lives of unbelievers by deepening relationships with neighbors, co-workers, friends, and family members that open opportunities to discuss matters of faith. Some observers of American

4.. Marshak, "Morphing," 9.
5. Kotter and Cohen, *Heart of Change*, 80.
6. Rendle, *Leading Change*, 8.

church life have recognized the signs of a new ecclesiological revolution in which churches are moving from an inward-focused, maintenance mentality of ministry to an outward-focused, mission-driven ministry, and they have been referring to these changing churches with a variety of adjectives: "missional," "emerging," or "incarnational."[7] A missional church understands itself to be on mission, not in the sense of traditional missionary activities, but as having been "created by the Spirit as a called and sent community to participate fully in God's mission in the world."[8] For our purposes here, missional change is defined as any strategic shift in congregational paradigms, attitudes, or structures in order to more faithfully accomplish the work of living out the reality of the Kingdom of God.

The history of the Church plainly reveals that missional change has been a normal part of life in every era since Jesus ascended to his Father. Not long after Pentecost, the predominantly Jewish Church was confronted by the reality that God's grace extended to the Gentiles, so changes needed to be made in order that Gentiles could be integrated into the life and ministry of the Church (Acts 15). In every era since that time, churches and ministries have been established all around this globe to reach people of every "tribe and language and people and nation" (Rev. 5:9, NIV) in fulfillment of the Great Commission of Jesus (Matt. 28:19–20). Many churches that were then established contextualized their leadership structures, worship patterns, and evangelistic methods to their specific cultural contexts in order that the people of their region or community might respond to and worship God authentically. As a result, the churches of the twenty-first century are vastly different from the churches of the first century. Indeed, the churches of Europe and Asia are different from the churches in Africa and the Americas. Churches that seek to reach out to the "millennial generation" are different from churches that embrace the Baby Boomers. The Church has continuously searched for bridges to the prevailing cultures and has adapted its structures and communication modes in order to effectively translate the Gospel to the people of those cultures.

Because this world and its inhabitants are in a state of constant change, it is essential that churches constantly change and adapt to the needs of their communities. If one truly pays attention, one will notice that, in even the most static contexts, last year's culture is perceptibly different from what one observes today. Most pastors no longer serve the same church or the same

---

7. See Guder, *Missional Church*, Kimball, *Emerging Church*, and McLaren, *Church on the Other Side*.

8. Van Gelder, "From Corporate Church to Missional Church," 426.

world they knew when they trained for ministry, which is why the greatest skill one can learn in preparing for ministry is not how to preach but how to discern that things are shifting. Continual, lifelong learning is needed to understand the people of the world today, and constant shifts in ministry will need to be made in order to adapt to changing needs. Church leaders cannot assume that because they have "read" the surrounding culture and have designed new forms of outreach to the community, they can sit back and coast through the next twenty years on auto-pilot. An awareness of the changing culture is the critical element of missional change. Churches and their leaders must be constantly and consistently moving beyond a maintenance mentality into a mission mentality, developing "a proactive ministry agenda targeting people and their life issues and concerns."[9]

While it is true that on occasion a congregation is more ready to embrace change than its appointed leader(s), a more common pattern, faced by pastors and congregational leaders generation after generation, is an unwillingness of the churches they serve to implement and embrace missional change.[10] Congregational resistance to missional change may occur on several different levels. The resistance may be spiritual, rooted in the theology and beliefs of the members and attendees of the church. Resistance may be cognitive, stemming from a lack of understanding or a failure to communicate the facts. Some resistance may be emotional, welling up from a real or perceived threat to an individual's well-being or an organization's survival. Sometimes resistance goes even further, manifesting itself in longstanding behavioral patterns of the resistor. Some resistance is relational, stemming from a lack of trust in the people who are proposing the change or in other congregational members. Because missional change involves a measure of risk, the trust of congregational members in one another becomes vital.

What many pastors and other church leaders often forget is that resistance is multi-dimensional, and so many of these dimensions of resistance have a great deal of overlap. Leaders of congregations may propose a missional change to the organization, and when the resistance starts, those leaders may assume that the resistance is only due to a lack of information. The lack of information may lead to anxiety and stress, triggering emotional resistance, and when information is withheld, the leaders are perceived as untrustworthy, which may lead to behavioral resistance. The leaders may launch a new campaign to inform the congregation of the benefits of the

9. McNeal, *Revolution in Leadership*, 25.
10. Caughlin, "Emotional factors."

Keep the Change

change, may design all kinds of instructional presentations and informational brochures to persuade the members of the need for the change, may preach and teach on the value of change, and may even do what we have done and research ways to overcome that resistance. All such efforts at increasing and improving communication may not succeed in overcoming the resistance if the other dimensions of resistance are ignored.

What is at the root of this resistance? Our argument here is that if an environment of trust were nurtured within local congregations, people would be more open to embrace missional change and, in fact, may find change irresistible.[11]

THE CHURCH'S HERITAGE OF MISSIONAL CHANGE

Even if an environment of trust exists within a congregation but congregants believe that a missional change initiative is contrary to biblical ecclesiology, they may resist and mistrust those who are proposing the change. Not all Christians have accepted this notion of the adaptation of a church to its surrounding culture; indeed, many have fought against it. Therefore, it is necessary to address briefly the biblical and historical rationale for the kind of missional change we are advocating here.

Many calls have gone out for churches to follow "the New Testament pattern" in their organizational structure and ministry styles. Since the Protestant Reformation, nearly every renewal movement in both Protestantism and Catholicism has claimed to represent "original" or "New Testament" Christianity in one form or another. Unfortunately, they tend to disagree with each other as to what that looks like. For instance, an article on the "Christian News and Views" website asserted that a prescriptive pattern exists in the New Testament book of Acts for all churches in all generations since Pentecost:

> In the infant New Testament Church they "continued steadfastly (persevered) in the apostles' doctrine (teaching)" (Acts 2:42). The apostles' teachings are recorded as part of inspired Scripture for us today. These give us the plan for the Church. These show and tell us how the Church functioned in its purest state. Could we follow any better plan today?[12]

---

11. Ken Hultman, personal communication, February 10, 2006.
12. Hulshizer, "Marks of a New Testament Church."

Condemnation is swift and harsh for "worldly" or "carnal" churches that have deviated from these so-called scriptural norms. However, this view raises a concern over which New Testament church provides the church today with a prescriptive pattern for church structure and ministry. The predominantly Jewish church in Jerusalem met in the Temple daily as well as in homes (Acts 2:46). The church in Ephesus, comprised of both Jews and Gentiles, met daily for two years in a rented hall (Acts 19:9). The church at Philippi met together near the river for prayer (Acts 16:13,16). The church in Troas met in an upper room on the first day of the week with sermons lasting until daybreak (Acts 20:7–11). The church at Colossae met in private homes (Phlm. 2). Anyone could point to any of these churches as being the prescriptive model for all churches of all times. However, because there existed a wide variety of ecclesiastical models in the New Testament, churches today are not bound to replicate any of them even if that were possible. There is no specific pattern found in the New Testament for the organization and ministry of the church, according to Brian McLaren:

> The new church does not view the New Testament as a "New Leviticus" – a law book of strict rules – nor as a fixed, detailed blueprint to be applied to all churches in all cultures across time. Rather, the New Testament serves as (among other things) an inspired, exemplary, and eternally relevant case study of how the early church adapted and evolved and coped with rapid change and new challenges. In place of a fixed structure that is to fit all, the new church advocates a flexible, adaptable, evolving structure that is developed to meet the current needs. The key word is adaptability.[13]

For those who insist that the twenty-first century church must follow the patterns of the New Testament churches, we argue that many of the New Testament churches, despite some inherent flaws and failings, were missional churches committed to change their course to move in the direction God wanted them to go in order to further live out the mysteries of the Kingdom of God. For proof of this assertion, one must look at a number of significant events in the life of the churches in the book of Acts. If the narratives in the book of Acts are viewed as descriptive rather than prescriptive, one finds followers of Christ who balanced a genuine care and concern for one another with an outward focus on reaching unbelievers in their own unique settings. The opening chapters in Acts describe a people who were continually

---

13. McLaren, *Church on the Other Side*, 23.

devoting themselves to teaching, fellowship, and prayer (Acts 2:42, 46). They were committed to each other financially, as many of them sold their possessions to provide for the needs of others (Acts 2:44–45; 4:32–35). They were continually proclaiming the Gospel of Jesus, both in the Temple and from house to house (Acts 5:42), resulting in the accusation by the Jewish leaders that they had "filled Jerusalem with [their] teaching" (Acts 5:28).

When the followers of Jesus encountered opposition to their message, they gathered together for prayer (Acts 4:24) and God empowered them to continue to speak with boldness (Acts 4:31). They experienced great joy as they recognized how God was working in their lives, and the community had a largely positive view of them (Acts 2:46–47; 5:13). The result was that multitudes of people came to faith in Jesus (Acts 2:47; 5:14; 6:1,7). Samuel Escobar comments that the growth of the first-century church "can be viewed as nothing less than a miraculous work of God, who used people wholeheartedly committed to Christ at the risk of martyrdom, sensitive to the direction of the Holy Spirit, and ready to use all avenues open for the advance of the Gospel."[14] The predominantly Gentile churches in Thessalonica had similar experiences as those of the Jewish church of Jerusalem. Paul gave testimony to the close relationships that were forged among these believers (1 Thess. 1:3; 3:6,12; 4:9–10), but he also commended them for their faithful proclamation of the Gospel (1 Thess. 1:8). The term Paul used was "sounded forth," which meant that the proclamation of the Gospel was like "the sounding of a trumpet or the booming of thunder."[15] It was a message that was clearly communicated and heard by the people throughout that region.

The Thessalonian believers shared the Gospel not only in their own city, but also in the entire surrounding region of Macedonia and Achaia (1 Thess. 1:8). The Thessalonian church, then, was a model church (1 Thess. 1:7), with a balance of inward-focused care for each other and outward-focused proclamation of the Gospel.

Those who believe that the purest form of the Church was in its infancy, as described in the New Testament, may perceive any proposed changes in the local church as unscriptural or unspiritual. Any perceived deviancy from the New Testament pattern for the church (whatever that may be) is rejected by those who hold to such a belief. However, scholars have seen for some time far less uniformity in the first-century church than

---

14. Escobar, *New Global Mission*, 39.
15. Demarest, *1, 2 Thessalonians, 1, 2 Timothy, Titus*, 47.

might be expected and that "much in our current image of early Christians is reflected from our own traditions and interests, more than from the early Christian documents themselves."[16] If anything, the variant forms of church polity arising from the Reformation illustrate vividly that sincere believers have not reached a consensus on one "true" or "pure" way to organize the community of the faithful. Rather, we come to see that God who was Himself incarnate has intended for his Church to be also incarnate in every culture with the Gospel, and this has proven to be a challenge for every church in every generation, including the first-century churches.

The author (of the book of Acts) structures his book around the Spirit's activities of ensuring that the gospel would be taken to all – everyone, all the way to the ends of the earth – everywhere, and that it would address all of life – everything. Jesus had made it clear that this was God's intent (see Matthew 28:19–20; Acts 1:8), but the church struggled to bring this intent of God into its shared practices. The early disciples struggled to live into the full reality of being a missional church. In the midst of this struggle, the Spirit led the church to live into its missional identity through the crossing of cultural boundaries and by developing fresh understandings, oftentimes in the midst of the church's reluctance. The leading of the Spirit in the missional church is characterized as much by disruption, change, conflict and adversity as it is by planning and strategy.[17]

This perspective should be very encouraging to many twenty-first-century church leaders. God is not calling his Church today to seek to replicate the work he was doing centuries ago, but to discover the unique work that he is doing here and now and to seek to be part of that work, regardless of how challenging that may be.[18] Many contemporary church leaders see the church of the apostles as being descriptive rather than prescriptive and understand that churches have a great deal of latitude in the kinds of changes that could be implemented.[19] Trying to accurately reconstruct any true "apostolic tradition" of the first-century church would be a very difficult task, since each church views the New Testament through its own theological lenses. All attempts at determining the parameters ordained by God which prescribe matters of order, structure, and practice within the church of every age, culture, and region are skewed by the cultural and

---

16. Cadbury, "Gospel study and our image of early Christianity," 142.
17. Van Gelder, "Missional Church," 445.
18. Blackaby and King, *Experiencing God*.
19. McLaren, *Church on the Other Side*.

theological orientation of the ones making such attempts. The church has been designed by God to adapt to changing situations, but every current practice and proposed change needs to be carefully examined in light of the Scriptures in order to verify that nothing would contradict what has been revealed. And in those areas in which one is not sure, the guidance of the Holy Spirit is given to discern where and how God would lead his Church.

Over the twenty centuries of its existence, "the church has moved from being a sect of Judaism to becoming an immense global family of diverse peoples, cultures, and languages who confess Jesus Christ as Savior and Lord."[20] Over those centuries, the Church has repeatedly swung from one end of the pendulum to the other, moving from an outward to an inward focus and back again. While many contemporary Western churches could be described as inward-focused institutions, such a description probably would not be true of most Latin American, Asian, or African churches, where the Church is growing at a rapid rate.[21] The disestablishment of Christendom in contemporary Western culture presents the twenty-first century church with a cultural context similar to that of the first-century churches.[22] Contemporary culture presents the followers of Christ with some unique challenges, and churches that are willing to embrace change may be most likely to effectively reach the surrounding culture with the Gospel.

THE CRITICAL NEED FOR MISSIONAL CHANGE

The problem of resistance to change has been prevalent within our own denomination, The Church of the United Brethren in Christ (UBIC). Tony has been a lifelong member of the United Brethren, and received his first pastoral charge at the age of 20. Paul joined the United Brethren in 1995 after a childhood in another denomination and pastoral service in a second. Both of us have remained with the United Brethren through subsequent years because, despite our occasional frustrations, it has had a wonderful heritage of missional change that we continue to be inspired by and tap into as members and leaders.

The United Brethren claim to be the first denomination formed on American soil, as opposed to those that were transported from Europe. The first United Brethren revival meetings were held during the German phase

---

20. Escobar, *New Global Mission*, 53.
21. Winter and Koch, "Finishing the Task."
22. See Escobar, *New Global Mission*, and Sweet. *soulTsunami*.

of the colonial Great Awakening, and its first attempts at organization followed the American Revolution. Despite schism and upheaval, it has held to its original statement of faith (written in 1789 and adopted in 1815), to a constitution adopted in 1841, and to standards of conduct for church members that have been largely unchanged for over a century. As one looks back over its rich history, it becomes evident that the UBIC began as an outwardly focused, missional movement, having been launched in the spiritual fires of the Great Awakening in the latter part of the eighteenth century. Clergy and laity from Reformed and Mennonite backgrounds united their efforts to spread the Gospel through the American frontier. Differences in theological outlook and ecclesiastical practice were minimized in order to do the work of the Kingdom of God. Many of the early pioneers recognized that their responsibilities to the world not only involved care for the souls of people but also included concern for the needs of the wider community. Social activism was very prevalent in the pre-Civil War years, and the church took strong stands against slavery, alcohol, and Freemasonry.[23]

Over the more than 200 years of its history, however, the UBIC became more inwardly focused with a maintenance (and in some cases, survival) mentality. Attempts in the 1880s to change the constitution resulted in a devastating split. Both factions laid claim to ownership of denominational property, resulting in years of bitter lawsuits. Those churches seeking to retain the original constitution found themselves in a fight for survival, having lost many of their church properties and denominational agencies. In the latter part of the twentieth century, the UBIC leadership recognized their growing marginalization in the culture and thus began to advocate for change on a denominational level. The church has since then been willing to explore new denominational structures and ministry models. This readiness to change has been evident in proposals to merge with like-minded denominations, increased involvement in church multiplication efforts, reevaluation of traditional theologies of ordination and ministry leadership roles, and an international reconfiguration of conference relationships. In addition, there has been a rethinking of the relationship between the local church and the denominational offices and ministries.

However, this denominational readiness to change has not filtered down to the local church level. From our own extensive personal experience, we observe that many of the local UBIC churches are functioning much as they did in the mid-twentieth century. For instance, Paul served

23. Blair, "Revivalism and Democratization."

three small UBIC congregations that each exhibited signs of resistance to change when he began his ministry among them. All of the congregations were over seventy-five years old, with largely aging congregants. While one of those congregations adopted changes in ministry roles and worship formats and grew substantially, the other two congregations settled into comfortable, maintenance routines. His current congregation began in the 1980s as a church plant and merged with another congregation in 2000. There have been trust issues in this congregation since the merger; it remains to be seen if the church will move into a growth pattern when the trust issues have been resolved. (Paul speaks more about this situation in chapter 2). Tony has served six United Brethren congregations (one of them a church plant) and found only one of the others to be open to the kind of changes that would move them out of an outdated ministry model. (Tony speaks more about this in Chapter 5.)

The United Brethren are noted here as a denomination somewhat typical of American Protestantism, with deep roots in revivalism, early expansion and growth, and periodic efforts to maintain cultural relevance by changing evangelistic approaches or church models. And, like many United Brethren congregations, quite a few other American churches in the evangelical or mainstream traditions are stymied to discover that missional relevance in the twenty-first century; indeed, many of their leaders have grown weary with the task of taking them there. So we draw from our own tribe and our own experience to illustrate how the broader American church might navigate the deep waters of missional change.

TEST YOUR OWN CHURCH'S READINESS

As we noted earlier, we argue that if an environment of trust is nurtured within local congregations, people may be more open to embrace missional change. A good deal of research has been done on the impact of trust on organizational change, especially in the workplace and other secular organizations.[24] Chapter 3 examines that research and seeks to determine its relevancy to pastoral ministry in the twenty-first century. Some may view trust as a "soft," unmeasurable entity, but Ken Hultman insists that trust is directly related to observable behaviors. He developed the Trust Scale to

---

24. A number of authors have influenced our thinking, including Covey, *The Speed of Trust*; Cloud, *Integrity*; Hultman, *Making Change Irresistible*; and Kouzes and Posner, *The Leadership Challenge*.

Leading Missional Change

assess "the degree to which behaviors associated with mistrust are present in a team or group."[25] A modified version of the Trust Scale was given to thirty-one congregations across the United States that represented a rather typical, random distribution of attitudes and behaviors regarding change. The results were analyzed to see if there was any correlation between levels of trust and mistrust in a congregation and the growth patterns of those churches over the previous decade. Chapter 6 summarizes the results of that survey and its analysis for the rest of us.

You might find it helpful to do the survey in your church and see how you stack up on the issue of trust and, by implication, on readiness for change. It's found in Appendix A.[26] The more people in your congregation that take it, and more they represent the entire population of your church, the more accurate your results will be. Please note, of course, that the congregational trust survey is just the first step in assessing readiness to change; we'll guide you through the further steps as you continue to read. Chapter 3 discusses the multiple factors that must be taken into consideration for a church to move from resistance to readiness.

---

25. Ken Hultman, personal communication, 8 June 2006.

26. Further information about implementing the Trust Scale in a local congregation and analyzing the results is available on the companion website for this book: www.leadingmissionalchange.info

PART TWO

Readiness

2

Paul's Story

A Church That Wouldn't Change (But Did!)

We were crushed and completely overwhelmed, and we thought we would never live through it. In fact, we expected to die. But as a result, we learned not to rely on ourselves, but on God who can raise the dead. And he did deliver us from mortal danger. And we are confident that he will continue to deliver us. He will rescue us because you are helping by praying for us. As a result, many will give thanks to God because so many people's prayers for our safety have been answered.
(2 Cor. 1: 8b-11, NLT)

RESISTANCE CAUSES PAIN

Here I tell you a story of my experience as a pastor of a church that had veered off mission, but by the grace of God has turned around and is now back on course. I wanted to write this book because of the enormous physical and emotional toll that resistance to change can have on those who are called to lead, and to offer encouragement to my fellow servants of Christ that God may have a miracle in store for you as well. But first, I would like for us to think about what the Apostle Paul (the *other* Paul!) went through in his ministry.

The Apostle Paul went through much adversity because of his commitment to Christ. But we also know that these sufferings that Paul endured did not destroy him. They did not quench his faith. They did not make him bitter against God. They did not make him into a whiner and complainer. He did pray for one of the causes of suffering in his life to be taken away, but God said "no." God wanted to teach him through the suffering that God's grace is all we need, and it is more than enough to enable us to endure the suffering. In fact, the sufferings deepened his awareness of his dependence upon God, and of his recognition of his need for God's grace to work within his heart.

NO SUFFERING IS WORTHLESS

In the passage from II Corinthians above, Paul explains that while we do face many difficult experiences, we also experience God's comfort. There is a strong connection between the sufferings we endure and the comfort we experience and share with others. The words used here for sufferings refer to a heavy burden, a crushing pressure, the feeling that everything is closing in around us and there is no way out. We have all felt that, haven't we?

But in the midst of the hard times of our lives, we experience the grace of God at work within us. He brings his comfort, which strengthens us to endure the suffering and gives us assurance that it will not last forever. God's comfort to us in the midst of our broken places is not for our benefit alone, but also for the benefit of our brothers and sisters in Christ. As we experience the grace of God mending our broken hearts, we are enabled to bring that same comfort into the lives of our afflicted brothers and sisters. God does a work *in* us so that he can work *through* us.

THE END OF OUR RESOURCES

Paul mentions some great trial he experienced in Asia – he does not specify the nature of that trial, even as he never specified what his thorn in the flesh entailed. Some have speculated what this trial could have been: the riot in Ephesus led by the silversmith, which caused his sudden exodus from that city, or the mob in Derbe that stoned him and left him for dead. While we cannot know for sure what this trial was, we know that it was devastating to Paul. It caused him to realize that he was at the end of his resources, and he felt as if it was going to kill him, quite literally. It is similar to the experience of someone who is drowning; in spite of her best efforts to stay afloat, she cannot keep her head up above water any longer. She begins to panic, and starts thrashing around in the water. All of the thrashing around exhausts her, she sees no rescue in sight, and she starts sinking for the last time. But those who have exhausted their resources are in the best position to be rescued. I was a lifeguard for a number of years. I know that if you are trying to rescue someone who is thrashing around in the water, it is very difficult to get him under control so that you can pull him to safety, without him pulling you down with him.

I love the way J.B. Phillips paraphrased this passage:

> *We should like you, our brothers, to know something of what we went through in Asia. At that time, we were completely overwhelmed, the burden was more than we could bear; in fact, we told ourselves that this was the end. Yet we believe now that we had this experience of coming to the end of our tether that we might learn to trust, not in ourselves, but in God who can raise the dead. It was God who preserved us from imminent death, and it is he who still preserves us.*

In other words, God allows us to go through times of brokenness, not to destroy us, but to bring us to the end of our own resources. All of his dealings with us as his children are meant to shatter forever any sense of confidence in the flesh and dependence upon our own resources. God works in our lives to enable us to fall completely upon him, to trust in him completely to preserve us from the dangers all around us, and to enable us to be what he wants us to be, and do what he wants us to do.

But I also believe that God wants to cause us to recognize our need for our brothers and sisters in Christ. Look at the last verse of this passage, again as Phillips paraphrased it: *"Further, we can trust him to keep us safe in the future, and here you can join in and help by praying for us, so that the good that is done to us in answer to many prayers will mean eventually that many will thank God for our preservation."*

BLESSINGS IN BROKENNESS

The congregation I currently serve in Carlisle, Pennsylvania, was once dying a slow death. I accepted a pastoral appointment to the church right after graduation from seminary. I had served other congregations over a period of 15 years, and had experienced growth and congregational health in most of those churches. So when I was given the opportunity to go to a small, struggling congregation to help it turn around, I thought I was ready for the challenge. I thought that I could dig into the tools and programs that had worked for me in other churches and help this congregation get back on mission and onto a growth track.

The church was started in the early 1980s as a church plant by the United Brethren's MidAtlantic regional conference. The denomination purchased a building for a worship facility and assigned a young pastor to serve. The church experienced strong conversion growth during those early years and a great emphasis was placed upon discipleship and spiritual growth. A number of people heard the call to ministry through their involvement in the church. The founding pastor and his family were well-loved by the congregation and many found it very difficult when the denomination transferred him to a larger church. Thus began a steady, downward slide in membership, worship attendance, finances, and conversions; as a result, the church shifted from a focus on mission to a focus on survival.

I was the third pastor to serve that flock. I had always joked in seminary that I wanted to be a church decline consultant: I could get your megachurch down to a tar-paper shack in six months or less! I could have people running for their lives out the doors faster than you could say the word "tithing." But church decline is not a funny matter. Church decline hurts. It hurts when people leave to worship somewhere else. It hurts when people we love walk out the door, and cut off contact with us. It hurts when we gather with other pastors, and they ask how things are going, and we can't even think of something positive to report. It hurts when everything we try to do to reverse the downward trend is unsuccessful. And believers are hurt when they get disappointed and lose their vision of how God wants to use them in ministry.

The most hurtful thing about church decline is the sense of personal failure. Pastors are kind of a funny bunch, in case you haven't noticed. We take credit for every victory we see in the church: "I had 5000 in MY church last Sunday." "I built the biggest church in town" (even though we never lifted a hammer or placed a single brick). But we also take personally every failure in the church. We are really good at assigning blame on ourselves when things go poorly in our ecclesiastical domain. But I like how Jesus responded when people tried to assign blame. Remember the question the disciples asked Jesus about the man born blind: "*Who sinned, this man or his parents that he was born blind?*" Aren't you glad that Jesus does not play

Paul's Story

the blame game? His response was, *"It was not the fault of this man or his parents, but this happened so that the work of God might be displayed in his life"* (John 9:3, NIV). It is never helpful to play the blame game, but we must trust the Lord to work out his plan in our lives.

We came to the point where we realized that if we continued on as we had been, we would only be dying a slow death. So our board agreed a few years ago that it was time to close the church, disperse ourselves among other Bible-believing churches in our county, and get on with our own spiritual lives. We set the date for our final service, and we put our building up for sale.

But how I thank God that his greatest blessings come out of our deepest brokenness. We were grieving the anticipated loss of ministry and the fellowship we had enjoyed with our brothers and sisters. We were grieving the lost opportunities to impact our community for Christ. I had been grieving for a good part of that year, even before the board made the decision to close, because I really did not know what God wanted me to do. Every year, every pastor in our denomination was scheduled to report to the conference superintendents. It was called a "pastoral audit." My audit that year was extremely painful for me personally, not only because of the decline in the church, but also because I had been dealing with incredible pressures and stress in my nine-to-five job (I was serving as a bi-vocational minister). When I met with the superintendents (one of whom was Tony), I was a physical and emotional wreck. And when I tried to tell them what was happening with the church, the floodgates burst, and I began to weep in their presence. They tried their best to encourage me, and told me that my ministry was not at an end, that they would move me to another ministry, but I truly felt that I was not going to be able to do anyone much good any more. I truly felt spiritually and emotionally dead inside. All of my resources were at an end. All of my strength was gone.

But God's greatest blessings come to us out of our deepest brokenness! Another pastor in town approached me with a simple request that we not close the church, but instead consider a merger of our two ministries. His congregation had left a local mainline church over theological and moral issues in their denomination and were meeting for worship in a rented facility on Sunday mornings. They were experiencing great growth and developing new ministries targeting children and youth, but they were hindered by the lack of a facility that could be used during the week. Both pastors found a good deal of agreement theologically and discovered that the two congregations were remarkably compatible. Like me, the other pastor was serving his congregation bi-vocationally. Our church owned its worship facility but had a declining congregation. The other church had a growing congregation but no facility, so a merger was a win-win solution for both churches. The congregations began meeting together for worship and within two months voted to become a brand-new church plant. The new church was not intended to be two separate congregations sharing a facility, but a true merger into one united church. This chain of events generated a great deal of excitement!

RESURRECTION IS NOT A ONE-TIME EVENT

I came back to life. God lit a fire in my heart, a new passion for ministry, a new love for his people, a deepened love for Christ, and an overwhelming sense of gratitude to God for raising this dead man to life again! And the spark which God ignited in me is being caught by his people in our new congregation, and God is giving us a fresh sense of purpose and an incredible sense of joy that this church that was dying is coming back to life and greater vigor.

We decided to name the new church "Bethany Evangelical Church." Bethany was the scene of the greatest miracle in the earthly life of our Savior, when he raised his friend Lazarus from the dead. God is doing a miracle in us. He is raising us to new life in him. Dry bones are coming together and coming back to life. He is implanting within our hearts a tremendous love for one another, which is overcoming any obstacles that may stand in the way of our working together for the sake of the Kingdom of God. He is giving us an extraordinary opportunity to do something great for his kingdom, which will impact our community in a positive way for him. When he prayed that we as his people would be one, united people of God, it was so that "the world may believe that you have sent me." And the greatest miracle we would be able to see today would be men and women, boys and girls coming to faith in Him.

Bethany was also a place where Jesus felt at home. He enjoyed sweet fellowship with Mary and Martha and Lazarus. We want Bethany Evangelical Church to be a place where Jesus will always feel at home, and where we will be able to freely fellowship with Him, and grow to love Him more.

The name "Bethany" also means "a house of healing for the afflicted." God is healing our hearts. He is breaking down barriers. He is mending the broken places in our hearts, and bringing his healing and comfort to us. And he wants to use us to bring that same comfort and healing to those around us who are afflicted. There are many people in our community who have been burned by church, who have been hurt by other Christians, who have been broken spiritually by their involvement with other professing believers. God wants to raise up a house of healing for the afflicted, a place where people of all backgrounds can come and be healed of their brokenness, a place where they can thrive under the touch of the Spirit of God upon their lives. As we sing together the praises of God, as we lift our voices united in prayer, and as we minister the Word of God, the Spirit of God is moving upon our hearts, and healing the broken places.

The two congregations blended together well in a strong atmosphere of love, acceptance, and mutual affirmation. Many service and fellowship events were scheduled the first two years to bond the congregations together. A good number of people who had not been part of either congregation before the merger heard of what God was doing and wanted to be a part of it. Small groups were started that strengthened personal relationships within the church. A "shepherd" ministry was also begun during those years to assist both bi-vocational pastors in providing pastoral care to the congregation and the "shepherds" and the "flocks" were organized with representation from both original congregations.

A number of significant outreach ministries arose out of the merged church, many of which were initiated by members of the congregation. A mechanic in the church had a vision of an auto repair ministry to help single moms, elderly widows, and those who could not afford repairs or basic maintenance. The ministry partnered with a community assistance agency that screened requests for help. Vehicles were provided for people attempting to move off of public assistance into the workforce. The ministry quickly outgrew the mechanic's own garage so a rented facility was obtained to accommodate growth, and they recently purchased a facility where they continue to thrive. Most importantly, the Gospel is being proclaimed through words and actions as the love of Christ is expressed in very tangible ways.

Other believers were mobilized to serve with their spiritual gifts. Congregants are constantly being challenged to be open to divine appointments to minister to people in their spheres of influence. Two members of the congregation were called to vocational ministry and enrolled in a local Christian college, even though both were in their thirties when they started. One is now serving as a pastor in a nearby church, and the other remains at Bethany, serving as Assistant Pastor of Christian Education and Youth Ministries.

However, not all was well in the new church. A strong, vocal minority was pushing for the construction of a new worship facility, and for a greater emphasis on building a stronger financial base. The pastors were pushing back, emphasizing the growth of God's kingdom and the necessity of incarnating the Gospel in our communities.

The issue came to a head with a teen suicide in the congregation in 2010. This tragedy prompted discussions with another local church on how to best reach at-risk teens with the Gospel of hope. An outreach event was held in the Fall of 2010 with BMX riding and skateboarding. We partnered with other churches on a joint Sunday evening event that we named "The Refuge." Bethany was able to purchase a renovated barn on eleven acres of land, which is ideally suited for ministry to children and teens. Many lives are being saved, and young people are being called into ministry as a result. The congregation moved out of our traditional church facility at the same time "The Refuge" was being established, and we moved our worship center to the barn. A number of families are now worshipping with us through the young people who have come to Christ. A youth praise band leads us in worship on Sunday mornings.

What does the future hold for Bethany Evangelical Church? Only God knows, but we have our confidence that he has wonderful things in store if we keep our focus on our mission and be willing to change how we work out that mission when God leads in a new way. As the Apostle Paul said to the Corinthians, so this Paul says, *"Here you can join in and help by praying for us, so that the good that is done to us in answer to many prayers will mean eventually that many will thank God for our preservation."*

3

Resistance Is Not Futile

Why Churches Don't Want to Be on Mission

LEARNING ABOUT RESISTANCE

IN CHAPTER 1, WE surveyed the current societal environment of the church in America, the heritage of missional change throughout church history, the need for missional change to be consistently and constantly undertaken in order for the Gospel to reach each generation and every culture, and, as an illustration, the challenges facing our own denomination. Strategic shifts in paradigms, attitudes, and structures may be needed to accomplish the tasks entrusted by Christ to his church. Based on past history and our own experience, some of which is related in Paul's narrative in chapter 2, congregational resistance to missional change is to be expected, but such resistance need not derail efforts at transforming a church. This chapter reviews what has been written over the past generation or so on the nature of resistance to change and explores the characteristics of the readiness needed in churches to embrace and implement missional change. The primary focus of this chapter is on the impact of trust or mistrust on readiness for missional change.

One might assume from the discussion in chapter 1 that the goal of a leader seeking to implement change within a congregation may be to react against the negative evidences of resistance that crop up. Research shows that a far more important priority for a leader is to foster a culture within the congregation that is creative and flexible, and permeated thoroughly with an atmosphere of trust.[1] Such a culture may be transformative, enabling many within the congregation to become initiators and embracers of change. When opportunities for significant ministry to the unchurched present themselves, a church that is ready to change can be out in the forefront, ready to seize those opportunities to grow the Kingdom. In the following sections, the various dimensions of resistance to change and the qualities needed for a readiness to embrace missional change are explored.

SPIRITUAL RESISTANCE AND READINESS

Resistance may be rooted in the theology of an individual or church. One issue that gets a good deal of attention in this regard is whether the church of the book of Acts is a description of how God moved in the churches of that era or a prescription for all churches of all times and locales. This issue was explored in chapter 1 of this book, and the conclusion reached was that Christ's Church is intended to adapt to its cultural environment while remaining faithful to the mission Christ has entrusted to it.

Belief in the unchangeableness (immutability) of God may also contribute to resistance to change. God is revealed in the Scriptures to be one "who does not change like shifting shadows" (Jas. 1:17 NIV), does not "change his mind" (Num. 23:19 NIV), and "remains the same" (Ps. 102:27 NIV). God asserts through the prophet Malachi that "I the Lord do not change" (Mal. 3:6 NIV). Most orthodox theologians also agree with the teaching of the unchangeable nature of God.

> God is unchangeable in his essence. He is unalterably fixed in his being, so that not a particle of it can be lost from it, not a mite added to it. In God there can be no alteration, by the accession of anything to make his substance greater or better, or by diminution to make it less or worse.[2]

The doctrine of the immutability of God raises the question of why he would expect his church to change if he, in fact, does not change in his nature. The dominant philosophies of the modern world teach

---

1. See Kouzes and Posner for a fuller treatment of this concept from a business perspective.
2. Charnock, *Discourses*, 319.

that "permanence and stability are in all cases preferred over chaos and change,"[3] so churches and other contemporary organizations would look upon change as something to avoid at all costs. A theology of change may give believers a greater understanding of how God works among his people. Some Scriptures seem to indicate that God's actions appear to be reactions to the actions and decisions of people, while others teach that God has everything planned out and works proactively for the fulfillment of his perfect will. The seeming paradox of these contrasting views raises the issue that if God adapts his mode of operations based on the current conditions, it seems to violate his immutability. If God does indeed change his ways of dealing with people, based on their particular needs, it would give great encouragement to leaders of churches to adapt to their cultural context in order to reach that population with the Gospel.

Thus, when James wrote, "God does not change like shifting shadows" (Jas. 1:17 NIV), he was not saying that God is immovable or unchangeable. The sun is constantly in motion, following the path prescribed for it. It shines with constancy. It is only our experience of the sun that changes, that warms us less in the winter than in the summer. The heat of the sun is the same, but what differs is where people are in relation to the sun. In the same way, God's love toward humankind is constant and unchanging. The difference is where people are in relation to him that affects their perceptions of what he is doing and how he is expressing his love toward them. Human sinfulness and misperceptions of God cause people to doubt his love and his goodness to them. God will always act toward humankind in conformity to his nature.

It is essential that our understanding of the immutability of God be set alongside of other things we know about God, particularly his omniscience and his calling. He is "not willing that any should perish, but that all should come to repentance" (2 Pet. 3:9 NIV). God knows exactly what every individual needs in order to come to faith in him and is actively engaged in calling men and women to salvation (Acts 16:14). The Father is actively wooing the sinner to repentance (John 6:44). The Son promised that when he would be lifted up from the earth, he would draw all men (all humanity, without regard to nationality, gender or race) to himself (John 12:32). The Spirit reveals to hearts the saving work of Christ in his death and resurrection (1 Cor. 2:6–16), and enables people to confess that Jesus Christ is Lord (1 Cor. 12:3). Because of the individual uniqueness of every human

---

3. Marshak, "Morphing," 10.

being, God does adapt his approach based upon all that he knows of an individual's nature and needs. God contextualizes.

This understanding of how God draws individuals to faith should be an encouragement to leaders of churches to explore new ways of reaching out to the unique needs of individuals and local unreached people. A key quality needed for Christ-followers to move from resistance to readiness to change is a deepened trust in God and a renewed or deepened intimacy with God.[4] Missional change is often messy. The old patterns and traditions of ministry are exchanged for new patterns and forms designed to better reach the surrounding culture. Church leaders may no longer be able to find security in the smooth-running operation of a church bureaucracy. Unfamiliar faces, skin tones, body decor, and accents may populate adjacent pews. The only hope of embracing the changes emerges as believers experience a growing, intimate relationship with the Heavenly Father and as they catch a glimpse of God weeping over the world and passionately inviting us all to repentance. Readiness to change is a natural outgrowth of a growing intimacy with God:

> Change should be the norm in light of our spiritual DNA. After all, we are created in the image of God and born of his Spirit and indwelt with his presence. The very fact that the church tends to become fixed in its ways is evidence of our lack of intimacy with the Spirit of God who loves to provide both new wine and new wineskins.[5]

The tasks entrusted to the Church are far greater than the resources and abilities of the people of God. God has entrusted the Church with "God-sized" assignments that have "God-sized dimensions."[6] The mission of incarnating the Gospel in every people, tribe, and nation seems daunting and overwhelming, but it requires a renewed sense of trust in and dependence upon the One with unlimited resources and upon the One who can empower the feeblest efforts. As the members of the Church believe that God is who he said that he is and he is able to do what he says he will do, the Lord of the Church is able to do extraordinary things in and among them.[7]

God is calling all of his people, including those in traditional churches, to enter into the adventure of being part of what he is doing in this

---

4. Minetrea, *Shaped by God's Heart*, chapter 2.
5. Burke, "Even Healthy Churches Need to Change," 43.
6. Blackaby and King, *Experiencing God*, 245, 271.
7. Ibid., 241.

world. Engaging this adventure, however, will require full surrender, total dedication, personal change, and a deepened spiritual intimacy in the lives of those who claim to follow him. God desires that all of his people would recognize that "no one can sum up all God is able to accomplish through one solitary life, wholly yielded, adjusted, and obedient to Him."[8] When a group of such people covenant to work together for the sake of a common mission, and are fully committed to do whatever needs to be done and to change whatever needs to be changed to fulfill that mission, the potential for radical transformation is multiplied. His will is done on earth, as it is in heaven.

COGNITIVE RESISTANCE AND READINESS

Cognitive resistance is the primary focus of much of what has been written about change and is the basis for most responses to resistance to change, both in secular organizations and in the church. Most leaders encountering resistance to their proposed changes respond by providing more information, as better and more frequent communication is generally touted as the solution.[9] The assumption is that if those affected by the changes would simply understand the rationale behind the proposed changes, they would come on board and support the new direction. Studies also show that people view leaders who provide information as more "trustworthy, honest, and caring" than leaders who withhold information,[10] especially if the information provided proves to be consistently credible over a period of time.[11]

Many leaders work under the assumption that people are likely to embrace a change once they understand the rationale for it. However, some scholars point out the need for transition, a period of time in which to psychologically reorient everyone within the organization to the change. We must remember that "change is external (the different policy, practice or structure that the leader is trying to bring about), while transition is internal (a psychological reorientation that people have to go through before

---

8. Ibid., 237.

9. See for example Fullan, Cuttress, and Kilcher, "Eight Forces;" Loup and Koller, "Road to Commitment;" Maurer, "Why Resistance Matters;" and Wanberg and Banas, "Predictors and Outcomes."

10. Wanberg & Banas, "Predictors and Outcomes," 134.

11. Rousseau and Tijoriwala, "What's a Good Reason to Change?"

the change can work)."¹² If this is true, what, then, needs to be included in a change process in order to help transition the members of our congregation into a fresh approach to mission? The literature shows that effective communication, alignment of mission and vision, and alignment of norms and values are vitally important in aiding such a transition.

Howard Gardner, who created the idea of "multiple intelligences," has argued that effective communication may result in the persuasion of the mind to adopt a new way of thinking when six factors (he conveniently alliterates them for us) work together. Change is more likely to happen when "reason, research, resonance, repetition, resources and rewards, and real world events" are integrated, and when "resistances are relatively weak."¹³ According to Gardner, when leaders are attempting to persuade their followers to adopt a new idea or to pursue a new direction, it is essential that they use reason (they help their followers to identify and assess all "relevant considerations") and research (they provide "relevant data").¹⁴ The new idea or the new direction must also feel right to the followers to the extent that they feel resonance (that is, they believe that "further considerations are superfluous").¹⁵ Effective communicators convey the message of a needed change in a number of different formats (what Gardner calls "representational redescriptions").¹⁶ Some helpful ways to do this include clear explanations of a proposed change, supported by charts, pictures, or graphs that depict the proposed change, or stories of people or churches that have implemented such a change.¹⁷ One can anticipate questions and prepare responses that reveal how the proposed change will address the needs of the congregation or impact the community; such dialogue may help to turn resistors into embracers of the change.

Resources and rewards may assist in effecting a change of mind.¹⁸ For example, a congregation may be more open to a new ministry if they knew that there were sufficient resources to implement the change. Perhaps a wealthy member of the congregation offers to fund the salary of a minister of outreach, so the hiring of additional staff would not pose a financial

---

12. Bridges and Mitchell, "Leading Transition," 31.
13. Gardner, *Changing Minds*, 18.
14. Ibid., 15.
15. Ibid.
16. Ibid.
17. Kotter and Cohen, *Heart of Change*.
18. Gardner, *Changing Minds*.

risk to the congregation. Rewards could also be the means of encouraging changes in thinking. When people are rewarded for a change in behavior or thought, they are able to see the potential benefits for themselves or for their organization, and thus they are more likely to embrace the change.[19]

Real world events can influence the acceptance of new perspectives or ideas.[20] For example, the condition of the economy could influence a person's or congregation's willingness to accept a new idea or resist it. When there is a downturn in the economy, a congregation may not be willing to invest its limited resources in a new initiative, but during a time of prosperity, they may be more open to that idea.

Resistance is the one factor of cognitive change that must be reduced if effective communication is to result. Because of long habits of thinking and deeply held perceptions, most of us "develop strong views and perspectives that are resistant to change."[21] Our internal resistance may be influenced or reinforced by a combination of factors."[22] For instance, people may be resistant to a new idea in proportion to the level of emotional commitment they may have to a cause or belief. People may cling to a belief taught to them in childhood and may feel disloyal to family or church tradition to abandon that belief. Public commitment may also contribute to resistance to change. If someone holds a view privately, it is relatively easy to change one's mind. However, once someone has made a public pronouncement of a point of view, "matters of pride and consistency push one toward hugging the theory, however discredited."[23] We have probably all been guilty of holding publicly to a view about which we have had serious internal doubts.

Personality factors may also contribute to resistance to change. Gardner notes that "the more absolutist one's approach to life, the more certain of one's opinions, the less likely one is to abandon them" but "it is far more adaptive to be low key, flexible, [and] curious."[24] Some scholars question the power of personality factors to hinder a change of mind. We might assume that certain people have a predisposition that resists change and that predisposition is itself unchangeable, since it is a personality trait, rooted in the past experiences of the individual. However, people often change their

19. Ibid.
20. Ibid.
21. Ibid., 17.
22. Ibid., 57–58.
23. Ibid., 57.
24. Ibid., 57–58.

minds and their actions if it is in their best interests to do so, regardless of personality traits. Jerald Jellison gives the hypothetical example of Lauren, who has a personality type that has a strong need for attention. As she is driving along the highway at 90 mph, she notices a state police car idling along the side of the road. Despite her strong need for attention, she does not flash her lights at the policeman but instead takes her foot off the gas and gently pumps the brakes to avoid attention that could lead to a fine. A few miles down the road, her engine starts acting erratically and she pulls off to the side of the road. She gets out of the car and begins waving her arms at the first policeman that she sees. In this second case, the attention of the police is in her best interests.[25]

This story illustrates the tendency of people to adapt their behavior to whatever may be in their best interests, regardless of personality type. When congregations are confronted with an opportunity to change, pastors and other church leaders quickly recognize the individuals who are the key resistors to change. Certain personality types quickly make themselves known and no one disputes their claim that "This is how I am" and "I will never change." However, "people act differently when the consequences in the present situation change."[26] If they can be shown how the proposed change will bring them certain benefits or that the failure to implement a particular change will have negative consequences for them, the personality traits or strong convictions that were declared to be unchangeable often find a way of bending.

Another essential ingredient in fostering mental readiness for missional change is to align the mission and vision of the congregation with its actions and decisions. The mission defines an organization's purpose and states the reasons for its existence, while the vision articulates the "desired future state that would fulfill the mission statement."[27] It is the role of a leader to "create a clear, compelling, and concise picture of the future vision and strategic direction"[28] and to make sure that the actions of the organization align with that mission. When an organization strays from its mission or vision, the trust of the membership in its leaders is diminished. In the case of a local church, the mission and vision are defined by the Word

---

25. Jellison, *Overcoming Resistance*, 25–26.
26. Ibid., 27.
27. Hultman, *Making Change Irresistible*, 156
28. Henderson, "Battle-scarred Reflections," 1.

of God, and the decisions that church makes regarding its direction must align with what God desires for his Church.

One of the essential keys to aligning mission and vision is that the congregation possesses clarity of purpose. The minds and hearts of believers are to be firmly rooted in the things that never change (the loving character of God) and focused on the things that always change (the needs of the community).[29] God has given the Church the ability to adapt to the changes in the surrounding environment so that local congregations might accomplish the unique purposes of God for them.

> A church sent into an ever-changing environment must be fluid in its capacity to adapt while maintaining a clear commitment to its unchanging purpose and God's eternal truth. Jesus assigned His mission to a Body with adaptive ability, not to a rigid organization.[30]

Most congregational leaders might assume that the purpose of every congregation is contained in the Great Commandment (Matt. 22:37–40) and the Great Commission (Matt. 28:19,20). However, the purpose of each congregation "is a local expression identifying the part of that universal mission an individual congregation senses as its responsibility."[31] Otherwise, there would be no need for multiple congregations in a community. So here's a radical idea. Let's agree that all ministries, all the things that congregations do, be regularly assessed to determine how they continue to contribute to the fulfillment of that congregational mission. And then let's discontinue all activities that do not enable us to fulfill our purpose, regardless of our emotional attachment to them. Why be so ruthless? Because churches must not cling to the past but engage in and embrace the present purpose of God. To know God is to know and trust the seasons of life, including the seasons of his Church.

> When church members see their church's best days as lying in the past, rather than believing they lie in the future, the events of yesterday's calendar come to hold magical power. Many struggling congregations seek to go back to the future, instead of valuing yesterday's experience as they faithfully walk toward tomorrow.[32]

---

29. Burke, *Healthy Churches*.
30. Minatrea, *Shaped by God's Heart*, 9.
31. Ibid., 102.
32. Ibid., 106.

Another thing needed for a congregation to foster cognitive readiness for missional change is to understand the underlying beliefs and values of a congregation. We all have them. In every organization, there are "fundamental social and ideological assumptions [which] are the glue that holds a group of people together and binds them in such a way that they can act purposefully."[33] But our priorities are not always in sync. There will always be conflicting values within every organization, and "the perpetual lot of institutions in modern democratic societies is flux and spirited disagreement."[34] That phrase characterizes many churches.

Many churches in our generation are indeed dealing with contrasting values among their members. Some Christians highly value authority within the church and see the church as the moral policeman who defends high standards in a culture that doesn't. Others value individual liberty and insist that no one has the right to tell them how they should live. Some churches value hierarchy, believing that God has raised up leaders who are to be respected and obeyed. Others value equality, insisting that everyone is equal in the church and no one has the right to impose his or her values on others. Some churches value tradition, wanting to continue doing things as they have always done them. Other believers value experimentation and are willing to try new forms of worship, outreach, and ministry for the sake of reaching the lost or experiencing more of God. Some churches value spectator-based, pastor-centered worship services. Others value a more participatory form of gatherings, insisting that all believers are to take an active role in the life and ministry of the church and to search for venues where such ministry can take place. Christians within local congregations often embrace conflicting values.

Ineffective or immature leaders of congregations often cave in under this kind of pressure "by either giving in to the demands of those who are most powerful or by issuing a command that represents their own will."[35] In other words, they submit or they attempt to dominate. Effective or mature leaders, on the other hand, strive to maintain a "values-based leadership" that creates "moral symmetry among those with competing values by creating transcendent values that provide a tent large enough to hold all the different aspirations, and in which all can find satisfaction."[36] In other words,

33. O'Toole, *Leading Change*, 169.
34. Ibid., 257.
35. Ibid., 258.
36. Ibid.

they find and hold fast to the glue that holds the various pieces together. Values-based leadership is not promoting mere compromise but creating (or discovering) an overarching mission that all within the congregation can embrace. Perhaps embracing of a mission greater than one's own comfort, values, or beliefs may be one of the most important keys to overcoming resistance to change.

The values and norms of a congregation must also align with its mission and vision.[37] Values and norms express the "how" for which mission and vision are the "what."[38] When there is a clear connection between the values a church espouses and the actions the people of the congregation practice, a culture exists that is ready and responsive to change.[39] Leaders must themselves embody the values of the congregation, showing by their actions the kinds of behaviors they want to be exhibited in the lives of the members and refusing to tolerate behaviors that are contrary to the church's norms.[40] This takes courage, but it is necessary. Pastors and church leaders lose all credibility when they fail to model Christ-like behavior. But they also lose credibility when they tolerate behaviors in other members of the congregation that are contradictory to the clear commands of the Scriptures or the character of God.

In the last few pages we have shown that effective communication, alignment of mission and vision, and alignment of values and norms are essential to overcoming cognitive resistance to change and fostering readiness for missional change. Understanding the rationale for change may not be enough if the leadership does not present a compelling vision of the future that is aligned to the mission of the church, and if the actions of the leadership do not align with the values and beliefs of the church.

EMOTIONAL RESISTANCE AND READINESS

One area of resistance that is getting a good deal of attention from researchers is the matter of emotional resistance. People may have all the information they need to agree to a proposed change within an organization, but the real problem they are dealing with is an emotional response to the

37. Hultman, *Making Change Irresistible*.
38. Ibid.
39. Schneider, "Why Good Management Ideas Fail"
40. See Hultman, *Making Change Irresistible*, and Kouzes and Posner, *Leadership Challenge*.

proposal. For example, a proposed change may trigger fear of the unknown or generate a profound sense of loss within an individual.[41] Some of this may be entirely unconscious and falsely attributed to other factors. As we have all doubtless experienced, even in ourselves, emotional resistance may stem from a variety of feelings: "loss of power or control, loss of status, loss of face or respect, feeling of incompetence, feeling of isolation or abandonment" or the "sense that [we] can't take on anything else."[42] When dealing with a change that involves a loss, whether real or perceived, people often experience the five stages of grief: denial, bargaining, anger, depression, and acceptance.[43] Other emotions that may work against change are "anger, false pride, pessimism, arrogance, cynicism, panic, exhaustion, insecurity, and anxiety."[44] Very seldom do we make decisions on a solely rational basis.

People may have an emotional resistance to change because it is perceived to disrupt their comfortable routines or traditions.[45] People in many different organizations are motivated by a sense of "complacency, driven by false pride or arrogance" to resist efforts to change.[46] Observers of the emotional context of American congregational life note that the "nature of the church organization, favoring stability and tradition, does not primarily encourage change initiatives."[47] Instead, modern churches emphasize sameness, closeness, warmth, and comfort.

> Difference, distance, conflict, and sacrifice are alien to this approach and therefore are to be avoided at all costs. Modern communities maintain a façade of unity and harmony by eliminating the strange and cultivating the familiar, by suppressing dissimilarity and emphasizing agreement. The traumatic and tragic events of human life are glossed over, ignored or explained away. Those who are strange – other than we are – are either excluded or quickly made like us. These images portray homogeneous communities of retreat where persons must be protected from one another as well as from outsiders, and where reality is suppressed and denied due to fear and anxiety.[48]

41. O'Toole, *Leading Change*.
42. Maurer, "Why Resistance Matters," 2.
43. Hultman, *Making Change Irresistible*.
44. Kotter and Cohen, *Heart of Change*, 180.
45. Caughlin, "Emotional Factors."
46. Kotter and Cohen, *Heart of Change*, 17.
47. Anderson, "Weight of History," 154.
48. Guder, *Missional Church*, 179.

To the contrary, missional leaders are usually people who are "uncomfortable with comfort," and such a frame of mind may elicit resistance within a congregation:

> The longing for comfort is powerful, and as a result, the commitment is not to break new ground, but to maintain what has been. Over a period of time, however, churches that continue doing the same things, maintaining the same organizational structures, keeping the same ministries, using the same methods for reaching new members, find themselves needing new resources. Missional leaders are not content to be ministers of maintenance.[49]

Missional leaders turn up the thermostat until people get hot and bothered. The primary task of a missional leader is "to maintain creative tension between the current reality and the preferred future,"[50] helping others within the congregation to become increasingly uncomfortable with the current state.

However, leaders must be careful how they go about creating such discomfort. Leaders of congregations must remember that people may resist anything that is perceived as forcing one's will over them, as "the major source of resistance to change is the all-too-human objection to having the will of others imposed upon us."[51] This attitude is a "you-can't-make-me-move deviance, driven by anger."[52] Besides the ineffectiveness of a domineering approach, the caution to leaders to not misuse their authority is also found in Scripture. The Apostle Peter warned the elders of the churches not to "lord it over" those who were under their care (1 Pet. 5:3), and Jesus told his disciples that it was not to be like that among his followers (Mk 10:43 and elsewhere). John Wesley said that church leaders are not to be "domineering," forcing their wills on the congregation.

For some, this creates a dilemma. While leaders must not be guilty of forcing change on a congregation, an unwillingness to try to move a congregation out of its comfort zone by implementing needed change may cause a local church to miss key opportunities for the growth of the Kingdom of God. Leaders face a delicate balancing act in creating discomfort while not appearing to be pushing people into changes for which they are

---

49. Minatrea, *Shaped by God's Heart*, 160.
50. Ibid., 169.
51. O'Toole, *Leading Change*, 15.
52. Kotter and Cohen, *Heart of Change*, 17.

not ready, but doing so in a timely manner so that unique opportunities for change are not missed.

Scholars see hesitance in implementing change as rooted in pessimistic attitudes and fear, and they warn that "there is a natural conservatism in all human societies that typically delays the acceptance of requisite change until it is too late."[53] Proposed changes may trigger emotional resistance if an individual does not see how those changes would particularly benefit him or her. The changes may benefit the organization but if they are not good for the individual, they often will be resisted.[54] This is dangerous for the Church, however. A focus on self-interest should not be the case for those who are seeking to live like Christ, who lived constantly for the sake of others (Matt. 20: 25–28). The consumerism that has characterized much of American Christianity in recent generations has made it difficult for both individuals and congregations to embrace change, even godly, missional change that is contrary to one's own desires and preferences.

We are called to something better than that. A Christ-follower who embraces change possesses a "resilient personality" that is hopeful and sees change "in the best light possible."[55] Some church members may put up resistance simply because they feel that they are being victimized by the changes that are being forced upon them,[56] but parishioners who are resilient see changes as opportunities for personal growth, whether those changes are initially labeled "good" or "bad." In local churches, it is vital that we help each other toward emotional maturity, which includes a hope-filled resilience when change is offered to us or even thrust upon us.

This is true outside the church as well. We have researched the question of openness to changes in the workplace and have found a number of critical factors for "creating employee readiness for organizational change."[57] These factors were self-esteem ("a high sense of self-worth"), a perception of personal control ("a view of life and situations as being under personal control"), and optimism ("a highly positive outlook on life"), which "together form a resilient personality."[58] These resilient individuals also have a higher confidence that they can enter a change process and emerge well, or

---

53. Ibid., 15.
54. Schneider, "Why Good Management Ideas Fail."
55. Wanberg and Banas, "Predictors and Outcomes," 133.
56. Kouzes and Posner, "Challenge is the Opportunity for Greatness."
57. Wanberg and Banas, "Predictors and Outcomes," 132.
58. Ibid., 132–33.

"an ability to handle change in a given situation and to function well despite demands of the change."[59]

However, resilience is not a golden bullet for a missional leader. Studies have shown that, while a resilient personality generally was willing to accommodate organizational changes, it did not make much difference in that person's perception that the changes were beneficial to the organization or its members.[60] Having a network of people to provide support through a period of change is also vitally important for emotional readiness for change. Research shows that "individuals with more social support tend to experience higher levels of mental and physical health during stressful life events" such as organizational change.[61] One would think that the social networks in a local congregation would provide the level of emotional support needed for readiness to change, unless those relationships are marred by behaviors that drive mistrust. Unfortunately, in many congregations the relational networks are very unhealthy, and it is essential that missional leaders reinforce those who are healthy and resist the temptation to unwisely spend their energies attempting to placate or satisfy those who are not.

It is not enough to persuade people of the logic of a proposed change. Something must happen within people that will grip them and make them passionate about a proposed change. Our research demonstrates that a number of emotions or character qualities may help to facilitate the acceptance of change within any organization. These include "faith, trust, optimism, urgency, reality-based pride, passion, excitement, hope, and enthusiasm."[62] It is wise to cultivate those who consistently display such qualities. Likewise, pastors need to be careful about how they communicate proposed changes to their congregations. If all that congregations hear from their leaders is a steady stream of negativity–all the things that are wrong in the church, all the things that need to be changed–there will be little enthusiasm for recommended changes. It would be better to communicate an impassioned vision of the future church and of confidence that the congregation has what it takes to implement that vision. The best future one can paint is one that is seen as emerging from what was best in the past, even if that former "best" is no longer what is needed.

---

59. Ibid., 134.
60. Ibid.
61. Ibid.
62. Kotter and Cohen, *Heart of Change*, 180.

BEHAVIORAL RESISTANCE AND READINESS

One form of resistance that gets a good deal of attention from congregational leaders and members is behavioral resistance. Behavioral resistance is evidenced by the actions people take, overtly or subtly, to sabotage a proposed change. Members of some churches may engage in open hostility toward one another, attacking each other verbally or physically. Other members may engage in what is known as "triangulation" or "hostility by detachment."[63] This occurs when chief critics refuse to voice criticism directly to the leader but instead talk to others in an attempt to win allies. When confronted or questioned about the criticism, the critics deny the criticism or claim that other people in the church may feel that way.[64] Members may withhold financial contributions from the church because they do not like the changes that are taking place in the congregation. Or members may leave the church entirely.

It may be helpful to remember that people have at least three options in deciding how to respond to change in any organization: "They can either leave the organization, resist the change, or try to adjust to it."[65] While behavioral resistance may take on many different forms, its net effect on a congregation may be very damaging to relationships and counter-productive to the kind of transformation God is inviting:

> People often escape situations they should face, avoid opportunities that could help them learn, and attack people with whom they should be building alliances. While escaping, avoiding, and attacking may allow us to deal with an immediate danger, which is their purpose, they do nothing to help us make something positive happen in our lives.[66]

So what do we do with behavioral resistance? Proactivity is a leadership quality that helps develop readiness for change in our organizations. Leaders do not wait until the behavioral resistance begins and then react to the circumstances. Rather, they have the foresight to look down the road and anticipate the possible negative reactions to a proposed change and work to prevent them. In a congregational setting, for instance, pastors may anticipate negative reactions from particular members of the congregation

---

63. Caughlin, "Emotional Factors," 28.
64. Ibid.
65. Hultman, *Making Change Irresistible*, 61.
66. Ibid., 16.

or board but conclude that a personal visit to those members prior to a meeting in which the proposal may be discussed may help them see the importance of the change. Some of these people may become allies instead of antagonists.[67] Again, this is possible only when one is dealing with individuals of a certain degree of emotional and spiritual health. Otherwise, a leader can expend all her energies tilting at windmills that will not be moved, no matter what.

Similarly, leaders need to develop a legitimate sense of urgency in their organizations in order to implement change, because without such urgency, "large-scale change can become an exercise in pushing a gigantic boulder up a very tall mountain,"[68] to use another image of futility. Leaders in the business community often desire to develop a sense of urgency in their employees to improve customer service. For example, one business videotaped an angry customer and the managers showed the tape to most of their employees. This made such an impression on the employees that they began meeting together to address the concerns of the disgruntled customer.[69] In a congregation, leaders should work at developing a sense of urgency in the hearts of the members. We all know that concern for the lost and a desire to reach those who need Christ should permeate the thinking of every believer. Perhaps congregations need to be exposed to "man on the street" interviews to be able to hear how people really view the church and what they really think about Christians in general. As long as presentations of the views of the unchurched are "visually compelling, dramatic, attention grabbing, and memorable,"[70] those presentations may have a powerful impact on the thinking of the people and create within them an urgency to implement missional change.

SUMMARY

Thus far we have examined four kinds of resistance to change: spiritual, cognitive, emotional, and behavioral. These are, of course, artificial and general categories, for resistance will often have its roots in more than one motive, and actions or attitudes that emerge from one of these categories will have impact on the others. Spiritual resistance to change will

---

67. Maxwell, *The 21 Irrefutable Laws of Leadership*, 47.
68. Kotter and Cohen, *Heart of Change*, 15.
69. Ibid.
70. Ibid., 35.

often generate resistance of the other kinds, for instance. They are helpful categories, however, in the sense that they give us knowledge and power to identify the issues at hand when such resistance is manifest. There is yet another category, however, and it both lies alongside and underneath the others, for relational resistance is, to some degree, foundational for the others. One may even break down spiritual barriers to missional change if one trusts the spiritual leadership of the person advocating for it. The next chapter explores relational change to a greater degree and then chapter 5 contains Tony's story about relationships and change dynamics.

4

Trust and Obey

How Churches Change to Be on Mission

RELATIONAL RESISTANCE AND READINESS

WE LOOKED IN THE last chapter at some of the reasons people resist change, specifically the roots and dynamics of spiritual, cognitive, emotional, and behavioral forms of resistance. But there is another factor that is at least as important as those mentioned thus far. Resistance to missional change sometimes stems from a mistrust of the ones who are proposing the changes or mistrust in other members of the group to which one belongs. This form of resistance may have nothing to do with the proposed change itself; an individual may fully support the idea, but because of a "personal history of mistrust," or "cultural, ethnic, racial, or gender differences" or "significant disagreement over values," he or she may react with resistance.[1]

Most of the research at hand confirms what we already know by intuition and experience: that an absence of trust may undermine attempts at strategic change within organizations, while a culture of trust often may accelerate and enhance change initiatives. The presence of trust is a powerful indicator of organizational health, and healthy organizations find change irresistible.[2] These conclusions are drawn from many studies of

---

1. Maurer, "Why Resistance Matters," sec. 3.
2. Michael Chase, personal communication, 11 February 2007.

the impact of trust on organizational change, most of which has focused on the business community and other for-profit and non-profit agencies.³ Surprisingly, however, little has been done to research the impact of trust on congregational life, which has some unique dynamics that these other organizations do not usually encounter. Therefore, the research we did for this book focused on the impact of trust on congregational resistance to or readiness for missional change.

What do we mean by "trust"? Trust may be defined as the expectation that an individual will do the right things for the right reasons, or the "positive expectation that another will not, through words, actions, or decisions, act opportunistically."⁴ While we all trust differently from each other—some deeply, others more cautiously, some broadly, others more narrowly—if we trust at all, it is likely we trust those who are known for acting in the best interests of others and who indicate through their actions that they truly care about the needs of others.⁵ And the converse is true as well. We mistrust those who have a track record of acting in their own interests or acting in ways that take advantage of others.⁶

How do we arrive at such conclusions? We watch how people act. Observable behavior has the greatest impact on our perception of the trustworthiness of others.⁷ Our trust is based upon the consistency or predictability of another person's observable behavior (Is the person "ethical, reliable, and dependable?") and upon the sincerity that we infer from their verbal and non-verbal communication (Is the person "genuine and non-manipulative?").⁸ Some scholars distinguish between "behaviors of character," which involve integrity, motives, and intent, and "behaviors of competence," which include "capabilities, skills, results, and track records."⁹ The distinction of behaviors of character and competence is important, as someone may be known for excellent character but may not have a good track record of results. By the same token, someone may have excellent results but not excellent character. We may choose friends solely on behaviors

---

3. See Covey, *The Speed of Trust*; Cloud, *Integrity*; Hultman, *Making Change Irresistible*; Kouzes and Posner, *Leadership Challenge*.

4. Lines et al., "Production of Trust," 223.

5. See Covey, *Speed of Trust*, and Hultman, *Making Change Irresistible*.

6. Covey, *Speed of Trust*.

7. Lencioni, *Five Dysfunctions*, and Covey, *Speed of Trust*

8. Hultman, *Making Change Irresistible*, 152.

9. Covey, *Speed of Trust*, 30.

of character, but in an organization with a mission to fulfill we usually look for something more. A proper balance of behaviors of competence and character is essential in establishing trust in any organization, especially in the church.

These behaviors may be describing someone you know and trust. Let's turn to an historical character with whom most of us are familiar as an illustration of what this looks like in real-life leadership. James O'Toole points to the example of George Washington, who inspired trust by the life that he lived:

> He had not promised the people he led much in terms of victory, glory, or abundance; he won their loyalty instead through deeds and by example. He asked no one to make a sacrifice that he himself was unwilling to make; he sought no financial reward for his service. The public's trust in him grew out of his manifest integrity; his ability to lead emanated from his willingness to serve. He imposed no doctrine on his people; instead, he came to symbolize their aspirations and their needs.[10]

Washington probably never demonstrated his trustworthiness more dramatically than when a few of his officers, frustrated with the apparent ineptitude of the Continental Congress, formed a plot to make Washington king. A couple of decades earlier, the young, ambitious George Washington would have found the temptation nearly irresistible. And even the more mature, responsible general would likely have recognized that his strong leadership skills might be more suitable for his new country than the ineffective leadership-by-committee that characterized Congress. But he remembered that he was fighting against monarchy and for liberty, and in an act of humility, not only refused the honor but chastised those who would think of such a thing. And this wasn't his only opportunity to prove his character. Later, when he was pressured to continue in the presidency to which he had been elected twice with nearly universal acclamation, he decided instead to retire to his farm. King George III of England, hearing of this, was astonished that any man could so freely give up power. "If he does that," the king declared, "he will be the greatest man in the world."

Washington's story, like those of so many others, demonstrates that one can earn trust by acting in ways that generate confidence in observers that one is acting in the best interests of the group, not one's self. Unfortunately,

---

10. O'Toole, *Leading Change*, 28. O'Toole may be exaggerating Washington's financial disinterest, as other researchers have noted the extravagance of his expense account.

gaining trust is not usually as simple as this. It is possible, for instance, for a leader to be unfairly perceived as untrustworthy, regardless of how sincerely he or she attempts to prove personal trustworthiness. In a business simulation with executives and senior level managers, one group was told that the team leader for the exercise was totally trustworthy, while the other group was told that the team leader could not be trusted. In the latter group, despite the best efforts of the team leader to convey openness and honesty, the "distrust was so strong that members viewed the manager's candor as a clever attempt to deceive them."[11] In one sense, we are too trustworthy; we form opinions on the character of other people not solely by observation but also through second hand judgments.

This illustration should serve as a warning to pastors and other leaders to guard their reputations and to focus on consistent behaviors that will build trust with their congregations or organizations, since the mere suggestion of untrustworthiness could create a climate of mistrust in a short period of time.[12] Because most congregational changes involve a degree of risk, it is essential that church members have a high degree of trust in one another and in their leaders. People are less willing to be cooperative to change initiated by those whose character is questionable or whose actions destroy or hinder trust. When leaders make decisions based only upon circumstances and not upon core values, they "will often encounter insurmountable obstacles on the road to leading change."[13] Such pragmatic leaders do not take time to build trust capital in the organization and often find that people are unwilling to follow them because of mistrust.[14]

Even if a leader starts a change process well, it is very possible to lose trust while it is in progress. The mishandling of resistance by leaders may cause an even greater resistance to a proposed change on the part of the followers simply because it causes a diminishment in the level of trust. Sometimes the resistance to a proposed change may cause the leadership to push for the changes even harder, which causes even greater resistance on the part of those impacted by the proposed change.[15] Other times, leaders might simply "react to symptoms instead of actively look for solutions that

---

11. Kouzes and Posner, *Heart of Change*, 246.
12. Ibid.
13. O'Toole, *Leading Change*, 99.
14. Covey, *Speed of Trust*.
15. See Maurer, "Why Resistance Matters" and O'Toole, *Leading Change*.

deal with underlying needs."[16] For example, if a leader deals with a verbal attack by threatening the verbal attackers, it may only "serve to increase defensiveness."[17] However, if the leader counsels those engaged in this behavior to uncover the root cause of the problem, it may help to diminish the resistance, and it is likely to lead to a perception of trustworthiness of the leader. A change process requires great discernment and often great patience on the part of a leader, for knee-jerk reactions will almost always create a more unhealthy environment than what already exists.

Most discussions of trust focus on the relationships between two people. Based on previous experiences and interactions over a period of time, trust is built between those two individuals. However, negative experiences and interactions can quickly destroy that trust. In most discussions of organizational trust, the focus is on a dyadic (two-way) relationship in which both individuals make judgments of the other's trustworthiness. However, recent research shows that there is a corporate component in the relationships of trust of people with one another. Interpersonal trust is shaped and impacted by a "complex web of existing and potential relationships" surrounding individuals.[18] It is rarely just about two people. Trust is the foundation of relationships in teams that work well together, and most churches function by "teams," even if they call them something else. When trust exists, people believe that their teammates have good intentions and they are willing to be vulnerable with each other.[19] When teammates do not have to worry about protecting themselves, "they can focus their energy and attention completely on the job at hand, rather than being strategically disingenuous or political with each other."[20] This corporate, broader dynamic of trust is readily seen in churches, as well as in many biblical accounts.

It is not difficult to find many examples of corporate trust and mistrust through the Bible. Moses' initial leadership of the Israelites was marred by mistrust as he sought to lead them in missional change. God's intention was to move the Israelites out of their condition of being slaves in Egypt to become God's treasured possession, a kingdom of priests, and a holy nation that would proclaim to the nations the One True God (Ex. 19:5–6;

16. Hultman, *Making Change Irresistible*, 93.
17. Ibid., 23.
18. Ferrin et al., "Interpersonal Trust," 870.
19. Lencioni, *Five Dysfunctions*.
20. Ibid., 195–96.

Ps. 96:2). When Moses first declared to the Israelites that God was going to deliver them from their cruel bondage in Egypt, they rejoiced (Ex. 4:31), but their rejoicing was short-lived when the Pharaoh increased their workload in response to Moses' demand. The Israelites not only questioned the competence of Moses, but they also questioned his motives, assuming that Moses was determined to kill them (Ex. 5:21). When Moses attempted to share with the Israelites the message of assurance that God gave to him, they refused to listen to him (Ex. 6:9). Only after the Lord began sending the plagues upon Egypt and not upon the Israelites did the people of both nations begin listening to what Moses had to say (Ex. 11:3,27).

The mistrust of Moses, however, continued on through the early years of his leadership of the nation of Israel. When Israel moved out of Egypt and was faced with the Red Sea in front and the Egyptian army behind, the people again accused Moses of wanting to kill them (Ex. 14:10–12). When God led them across the Sea on dry land, they believed in the Lord and in his servant Moses (Ex. 14:22). That trust again was short-lived, as the Israelites soon faced a shortage of food (Ex. 16:2–3) and a shortage of water (Ex. 17:2–3). Both of these deficits again elicited the accusation that Moses was determined to kill the entire nation, but in all these cases, God revealed his power in providing miraculously for the people.

God established Moses' leadership of the people by revealing to all that they were to listen to Moses because Moses listened to God. God appeared in a dense cloud in plain sight of the people of Israel and they could hear God speaking with Moses. God told Moses that he did this "so that the people will hear me speaking with you, and *will always put their trust in you*" (Ex. 19:9; NIV, emphasis added). While no historian has ever disputed the authority that Moses exerted over the Jewish people, the sharp reader will note that it took supernatural intervention to establish Moses' leadership of the nation. What about those situations in which such dramatic supernatural action appears unlikely?

Another powerful example of dyadic trust may be found in the Old Testament story of Nehemiah. While this story involves the favor of God, it is primarily a story of a leader exercising non-supernatural wisdom. There was an apparent lack of hesitancy in the response of King Artaxerxes to Nehemiah's request to be sent to the land of Judah to rebuild Jerusalem. The Scriptures attributed this lack of hesitancy to "the gracious hand of God" in answer to Nehemiah's prayer (Neh. 2:4, 8). God changed the heart of the king, so that he would be agreeable with Nehemiah's request. However, it should be pointed out how impossible this lack of hesitancy would seem from a purely human standpoint. Nehemiah was a servant in the king's household, the "cupbearer" of the king. He was an exile living in Babylon, far from his native country. His homeland was known to be a hotbed of sedition and rebellion, rising up against all foreign invaders (Ezra 4:11–16), so Nehemiah's motives could have been questioned. Nevertheless, he asked not only to be allowed to return to Jerusalem to rebuild the city but also for the resources that would be needed to accomplish the task. Nehemiah's request involved a great expense to the king, as well as the loss of Nehemiah's services for an extended period of time, possibly as long as twelve years (Neh. 2:1; 13:6). The request to rebuild the city of Jerusalem also meant that Nehemiah was aspiring to be made governor of Judah, since those who rebuilt cities in ancient times had great authority and were revered by the inhabitants.[21]

Explaining the graciousness of this king in granting this request without reservation would be very difficult. However, the willingness of the king may have been due, in part, to the trust that Artaxerxes had in Nehemiah. The king's cupbearer was not an incidental position in the court, a "nice-to-have" employee for really rich kings. The cupbearer was the one who tasted the king's wine and guarded the royal apartments. If someone slipped poison into the king's cup, the cupbearer died instead of the king. The king recognized in Nehemiah someone who was willing to die for him, which took trust to a much higher level. Such trust is the kind of trust that is needed in congregations and relationships, the kind of trust that goes much further than taking care of people if they take care of us.

> If [people] are objects, then they are to be used and manipulated, even treated well, as a means to an end. But, if they are valued as people, then they are to be treated as we treat the ones who really do matter to us, with care, concern, and intent to do good, not harm. We treat them as we would want to be treated.[22]

Can we find this deep trust in a group larger than two individuals? The Bible includes the marvelous story of the resolution of a dispute between Hellenistic Jews and Hebraic Jews during the early years of the first-century church. This story wonderfully illustrates the power of corporate trust in implementing change. In Acts 6, the account is given of a dispute that arose over the distribution of assistance to widows. The Hellenistic Jews believed that their widows were being neglected and the dispute came to the attention

---

21. Clines, *Ezra, Nehemiah, Esther*.
22. Cloud, *Integrity*, 80–81.

of the apostles. The decision of the apostles was startling, or at least is startling to our own time, for seldom do we see this kind of trust in twenty-first-century congregations. They gave instructions to the believers to choose seven men who were to be placed in charge of the distribution of assistance, *and the church selected seven men who all had Hellenistic names*. It appears that these early believers were willing to entrust the entire ministry into the hands of those who believed that their widows were being overlooked, which required a great deal of trust on the part of the Hebraic believers. They believed that their Hellenistic brothers would not take advantage of this situation and begin acting wrongly toward the Hebraic widows.

Trust, as seen in these biblical examples, is built over a long period of time, through multiple interactions between the trustor and the trustee (whether an individual or an organization). But here's the rub: trust may be ruined very quickly.[23] Breaches of trust are "difficult to restore because people erect psychological barriers around their relationship with each other to protect themselves from getting hurt."[24] The only way to overcome those psychological barriers and rebuild trust is by focusing one's energies on the behaviors that help to build trust and actively resisting those behaviors that may result in further mistrust. Not all losses of trust are permanently irreparable but trust may be rebuilt over time.[25]

MEASURING TRUST IN YOUR CHURCH

The diagnosis of trust and mistrust is a first step toward moving a group of people toward interpersonal and organizational effectiveness.[26] Studies have shown that organizations with high levels of mistrust have diminished levels of commitment and productivity from their members because "when trust is low, people focus on protecting themselves from each other instead of focusing on accomplishing organizational goals."[27] A helpful tool is available to organizational leaders to assist in the diagnosis of trust and mistrust. As noted earlier, trust and mistrust in organizations are directly related to observable behaviors.[28] Hultman's Trust Scale is designed for the business and non-profit

23. Lines et al., "Production of Trust."
24. Hultman, *Making Change Irresistible*, 155.
25. Ibid.
26. Hultman and Gellerman, *Balancing Individual and Organizational Values*.
27. Ibid., 77.
28. Covey, *Speed of Trust*, and Lencioni, *Five Dysfuctions*.

communities to measure the degree to which behaviors fostering mistrust are present in organizations.[29] Each member of an organization being researched is given a copy of the Trust Scale and asked to evaluate how frequently he or she has observed each of the thirty behaviors addressed on the survey. If a particular behavior has almost never been seen in the interpersonal relationships within the workgroup, he or she ranks that behavior as a "4" but if that behavior has almost always been seen, he or she ranks that behavior as a "0." Mid-rankings of "frequently," "occasionally," or "rarely" are given a score of "1," "2," or "3" respectively. Scores are then tabulated, providing a mean score for the group. Through the anonymous completion of the Trust Scale by coworkers and team members, the behaviors most contributing to mistrust can be identified and a plan developed which addresses those behaviors and builds trust in that particular group.[30]

As noted earlier, the behaviors addressed in Hultman's Trust Scale include many different types. A number of behaviors involve breakdowns in communication (e.g., gossip, withholding information, and inconsistent messaging). Other behaviors relate to reactions to errors (e.g., blaming others and making excuses), while other behaviors have to do with the provision of feedback (e.g., criticism and put downs). Some behaviors involve building group cultures that exclude others (e.g., formation of cliques), while others revolve around corporate decision-making (e.g., political maneuvering, unilateral decisions, and springing surprises). Most damaging are behaviors that promote self-interest over corporate interests (e.g., seeking win-lose outcomes and undercutting others) and active aggression (e.g., attacking others and seeking revenge). Many of these behaviors have already been referenced in this chapter as contributing to mistrust in organizations.

The prevalence of the behaviors that foster mistrust is very significant for church leaders in that these behaviors are not merely negative characteristics of local church relationships but they are also contrary to the Spirit of Christ and violations of biblical commandments and principles.[31] The Bible is full of warnings about how believers communicate with each other, how they treat each other when one has failed, and how they provide accountability to each other. The Scriptures are clear in teaching followers of

---

29. Ken Hultman, personal communication, 11 February 2006.

30. Hultman, *Making Change Irresistible*.

31. For a table showing how the behaviors tracked in Hultman's Trust Scale are violations of biblical commands or principles, go to the companion website, www.leadingmissionalchange.info

Christ that concern for fellow Christians always has precedence over self-interests, since they are to have the same attitudes as the Lord Jesus himself. There is no question that Jesus taught his followers not to act aggressively toward one another or to seek revenge but rather to be gentle and forgiving of one another. Because the behaviors tracked in the Trust Scale are so significant to congregational life, it was chosen as the research instrument for the congregational survey we conducted.

BUILDING (OR REBUILDING) TRUST IN YOUR CHURCH

Confronting reality

Over the next few pages, the behaviors highlighted in Hultman's Trust Scale are examined in light of the Scriptures and other literature, along with the contrasting behaviors that may foster trust. We start with the hard stuff. Building trust requires leaders to "confront reality," which means "taking the tough issues head-on . . . sharing the bad news as well as the good, naming the 'elephant in the room,' addressing the 'sacred cows,' and discussing the 'undiscussables.'"[32] Too often, because of a desire for unity and peace, pastors and church leaders may not raise issues that they know could create conflict within the church. However, these leaders lose credibility among church members who recognize that important issues are not being addressed. For example, pastors may not want to talk publicly about budget shortfalls or failure to reach goals because they do not want to discourage the flock. However, this failure to discuss the issues undermines trust because people want to know the truth, even if it hurts.

The diagnosis of the level of mistrust within any organization is the first step toward enabling that organization to rebuild trust. Mistrust does not go "away by itself and does not fade with time."[33] Mistrust must be confronted directly because "unless trust issues are brought to the surface and dealt with, they remain deeply ingrained, negative aspects of culture."[34] Hultman's Trust Scale is a valuable instrument for use in a congregation to bring the negative actions out into the light, to cause people to recognize

---

32. Covey, *Speed of Trust*, 185.
33. Hultman and Gellerman, *Balancing Individual and Organizational Values*, 77.
34. Ibid.

the reality of the situation in which they find themselves, and to seek repentance for damaging behaviors.

However, it is not enough for a congregation to merely talk about trust issues; members need to focus on practicing behaviors that build trust. People may be prone to condemn the actions and behaviors that foster mistrust, especially as they have been shown to be contrary to the principles of the Bible and contrary to the Spirit of Christ, but it is far more important for parishioners to concentrate on living the behaviors that build trust in one another. The glory of the Gospel is that Christians need not try on their own or with their own resources to become the kind of people they ought to be but they may seek supernatural power to behave in ways that will foster trust.

Behaviors relating to communication

The first question in Hultman's Trust Scale investigates the issue of how often people "say one thing but do another." This behavior has to do with words that are inconsistent with one's actions, which is the essence of hypocrisy. Jesus had some of his harshest words for hypocrites. In one situation, he described them as people who are beautiful on the outside but are "full of dead men's bones on the inside" (Matt. 23:27–28, NIV). It is readily apparent how inconsistent words and actions would engender mistrust within any organization.[35] The behaviors that build trust are speaking the truth, letting one's words be consistent with one's actions (Col. 3:9), "being real and genuine, and telling the truth in a way people can verify."[36]

Broken promises undermine trust within organizations (Trust Scale question 2). The writer of Ecclesiastes warned his readers that "it is better not to vow than to make a vow and not fulfill it. Do not let your mouth lead you into sin" (Eccles. 5:5–6, NIV), clearly stating that when promises are made, they are to be kept. Paul reminded the Corinthians of a promise of financial aid for the poor in Jerusalem and told them: "Now finish the work, so that your eager willingness to do it may be matched by your completion of it, according to your means" (2 Cor. 8:11, NIV). Delivering results and keeping commitments build trust in organizations. The business world and congregational life are filled with many people who "make all kinds of fantastic presentations and exciting promises of all the wonderful results they

---

35. Ferrin et al., "Interpersonal Trust."
36. Covey, *Speed of Trust*, 153.

are going to achieve. But when it comes down to it, they either never deliver or deliver far short of what they promise."[37]

Business leaders agree that it is far better "to give the best opportunities to the big producer who doesn't talk instead of the big talker who doesn't produce."[38] In a survey of leaders for the World Economic Forum, the number one reason given for a lack of trust in leaders was "not doing what they say."[39] If people are faithful in keeping the promises they make, it will build greater trust in their relationships.[40]

Two of the questions in Hultman's Trust Scale relate to communication involving controversial issues or bad news, examining the prevalence of inconsistent messaging (question 3: "say one thing to one person and something else to another person"), and artificial harmony (question 4: "pretend to agree with others"). Leaders need to avoid developing an artificial harmony in organizations because of a fear of conflict by glossing over the conflicts and never pointing out areas of disagreement in order that they might keep peace.[41] Some people have a habit of modifying their messages to suit the particular audience they are addressing, telling someone what they think the other wants to hear, and it can result in inconsistent messaging throughout the organization.[42] This matter of honesty is a critical issue in congregational relationships. Christians should always be known for honesty, willing to speak the truth to others, even if it is not to the listener's liking or contrary to the listener's views. Paul wanted the Corinthians to be aware that what he was in his letters was the same person he was when he would be with them, and the message he was giving in the letters would be the same message he would deliver in person (2 Cor. 10:11). Paul also told the Ephesians: "each of you must put off falsehood and speak truthfully to his neighbor" (Eph. 5:25, NIV). Absolute honesty builds trust within organizations, especially churches.[43]

---

37. Ibid., 172.
38. Ibid., 173.
39. Study cited by Covey, *Speed of Trust*, 217.
40. O'Toole, *Leading Change*.
41. Chase, "Covert Processes."
42. Lencioni, *Five Dysfunctions*. See also Ferrin et al., "Interpersonal Trust" and Henderson, "Battle-Scarred Reflections"
43. Covey, *Speed of Trust*, and Kotter and Cohen, *Heart of Change*.

Honesty in communicating bad news also fosters trust. Leaders are "to tell the truth and to leave the right impression,"[44] but leaders who are less than honest when communicating bad news foster mistrust in their organizations. For example, a study of business managers revealed that when they tried to put the best spin on what had been accomplished, they "overplayed the positives to such an extent that they became unbelievable."[45] Their direct reports recognized that what was being communicated was not completely true to the situation. As a result, when genuine accomplishments were highlighted, people were not sure if they could believe them. "When their credibility collapsed, even a legitimate win was viewed with suspicion."[46] Likewise, in the life of a congregation, when pastors consistently attempt to put the best "spin" on negative news or to overplay the accomplishments of a local church, they undermine their credibility, often resulting in mistrust and suspicion.

Another behavior relating to communication is the discrediting of others (question 5). There is a powerful illustration of discrediting others in the Old Testament. Absalom wanted to be king in place of his father, David, so he put himself in a place where those with disputes would pass. He sympathized with them that there was no one in the king's service who was able to help them settle the dispute. He followed up with the boast, "If only I were appointed judge in the land. Then everyone who has a complaint or case could come to me and I would see that he gets justice" (2 Sam.15: 4, NIV). By discrediting his father's leadership, he was hoping that he could turn the hearts of the Israelites in his direction and, for a time, it worked. By running others down, trust is undermined. Instead of discrediting others, people should celebrate accomplishments, show appreciation for the contributions of others, and believe the best of others.[47]

Another communication behavior that fosters mistrust is withholding information from others (question 7). When information is not adequately communicated to a congregation in a timely manner or secrets are purposely kept, people view their leaders with suspicion.[48] However, timely, adequate communication causes followers to assume that their leaders are

---

44. Covey, *Speed of Trust*, 137.
45. Kotter and Cohen, *Heart of Change*, 139.
46. Ibid.
47. Kanter, "Enduring Skills."
48. Covey, *Speed of Trust*.

trustworthy.[49] Enough information needs to be shared with everyone in the group to keep people moving in the same direction.[50] A biblical example of this principle is shown through the apostle Paul, who wrote in many of his epistles that he did not hesitate to proclaim to them everything they needed to know to become the people God wanted them to be. He said to the Corinthians, "We have spoken freely to you, Corinthians, and have *opened wide our hearts to you*" (2 Cor. 6:11; NIV, emphasis added). In the same way, twenty-first century pastors and church leaders should open their hearts wide to their congregations and share with them everything they need to know in order to enable all the members to accomplish the unique mission God has given them.

Gossip is another communication behavior that breeds mistrust (question 10). There are numerous passages in the Bible condemning the sin of gossip, such as: "A gossip betrays a confidence, so avoid a man who talks too much" (Prov. 20:19, NIV). People do not trust those who talk about others when those individuals are not present because they can be reasonably sure that when they themselves are not present, they will be the topic of conversation.[51] When people betray the confidences of others, people hesitate to entrust any confidences in them for fear they will be betrayed as well. Of all people, Christians should be known as people who honor confidential information. Using words to build up rather than tear down, praising others, and sharing positive things about others can build trust quickly within any organization.[52]

The distortion of the words of others also breeds mistrust within organizations (question 13). This principle comes through in the Scriptures, when Peter wrote of those who distorted the words of Paul as well as other Scriptures (2 Pet. 3:16). The original word used here is translated "twist" or "torture" and means to misinterpret words to make them "support [one's] own misguided views."[53] No one wants his or her words twisted to mean something that was never intended. People want their words and their views understood and communicated accurately to others.[54]

---

49. See Wanberg and Banas, "Predictors and Outcomes" and Lines et al., "Production of Trust."

50. See Covey, *Speed of Trust*, Kouzes and Posner, *Leadership Challenge*, and Lencioni, *Five Dysfunctions*.

51. Cloud, *Integrity*.

52. Covey, *Speed of Trust*.

53. Bauckham, *Jude, 2 Peter*, 332.

54. Cloud, *Integrity*.

A vital skill which may help to build trust is the ability to listen carefully to the ideas and concerns presented by others. Scholars believe that if "people feel that their ideas are listened to and accepted, they are more likely to recommend innovative and 'out-of-the-box' solutions."[55] People want their leaders to listen to them, even if their leaders do not agree with them. "We trust people who we think hear us, understand us, and are able to empathize with our realities as well as their own."[56] There are two sides to listening that builds trust: "to genuinely seek to understand another person's thoughts, feelings, experience, and point of view" and "to do it first (before you try to diagnose, influence, or prescribe)."[57]

Behaviors relating to dealing with mistakes

Three of the questions in the survey refer to the manner in which mistakes are handled. Focusing on the mistakes of other people (question 6) is one behavior that breeds mistrust. Some congregations have "blame historians" who keep track of every mistake that everyone makes, and do not hesitate to bring those failures up for review. Paul said, "Love keeps no record of wrongs" (1 Cor. 13:5, NIV). If churches want to build trust, they should focus on the positive contributions of each member rather than on failures and limitations.[58] And congregational leaders need to find the courage to set the tone in such matters.

Making excuses for mistakes breeds mistrust in congregations (question 8). The most amusing excuse found in the Bible was the explanation Aaron gave to Moses about the golden calf. He told Moses, "I told them, 'Whoever has any gold jewelry, take it off.' So they gave me the gold, and I threw it into the fire, and out came this calf" (Ex. 32:24, NIV). While no one, to our knowledge, has attempted an excuse as unbelievable as this one, people do try to cover over their mistakes with all kinds of rational and irrational excuses. One example is the creative use of the passive voice: "The milk was spilt" rather than "I spilled the milk." Taking responsibility for mistakes can actually breed increased confidence, but creating or offering feeble excuses for mistakes breeds mistrust.[59]

55. Cornelius, "Leading a Culture Ready for Change," sec. 3.
56. Cloud, *Integrity*, 52–53.
57. Covey, *Speed of Trust*, 208.
58. Ibid.
59. Ibid.

Even worse, blaming others for one's mistakes results in suspicion and mistrust (question 18). The classic illustration of this was Adam's blaming of Eve (and ultimately God) for his disobedience in eating the forbidden fruit. Adam said, "The woman *you* put here with me – she gave me some fruit from the tree and I ate it" (Gen. 3:12, NIV, emphasis added). Yes, congregational leaders do need to hold each other accountable for decisions and actions that are taken, but they also need to take personal responsibility for mistakes where appropriate in order to build trust in their churches.[60]

A behavior that helps to build trust is making restitution for mistakes that are made. Those who "cover up" or try to hide mistakes, "deny or justify wrongs, rationalize wrongful behavior, or fail to admit mistakes until [they are] forced to do so" destroy the trust of others in an organization or a relationship.[61] The dismissal in 2006 of a Colorado pastor is a powerful illustration. He had been accused of drug abuse and involvement with a homosexual prostitute, but he denied those charges until he was forced to admit to them by the magnitude of the evidence against him. The leadership of that church at that point had no choice but to relieve him of his position as pastor and to send him into a restoration process.[62]

Behaviors relating to the provision of feedback

Three of the questions in the Hultman Trust Scale relate to how feedback is given to people within the congregation. Putting others down (question 17), criticizing (question 22), and giving more negative feedback than positive feedback (question 25) all are wrong ways of providing feedback to people.[63] Paul warned the Ephesians that they should not "let any unwholesome talk come out of [their] mouths, but only what is *helpful for building others up*, according to their needs, that it may *benefit* all who listen" (Eph. 4:29; NIV, emphasis added). When changes need to be made in a church, it is not helpful for those seeking to implement the changes to be negative and critical of the congregants. People need positive feedback and when it is conveyed with respect and an optimistic attitude, it helps them to develop into the kinds of people who can bring the most benefit

---

60. Ibid.
61. Ibid., 160.
62. Olsen, "I am guilty."
63. Hultman, *Making Change Irresistible*.

to the congregation.[64] Often the most trust-inspiring thing a leader can say, if done with honesty, is "I believe in you, and am proud to be your pastor."

Behaviors involving exclusive relationships

One of the survey questions focused on the forming of cliques (question 12). Christians have a tendency to gravitate toward those who are like them, and churches often form and grow through what are called "homogenous relationships."[65] In fact, a generation or so ago this was recommended as a valid and effective church growth strategy, until critics warned that such behaviors only perpetuated the racial and ethnic segregation that has so long characterized American Christianity. While many churches advertise themselves to be "friendly" churches, often their friendliness may be limited to the people who resemble them. Those who do join a church often gravitate to those who have similar life circumstances or interests, thus forming cliques.

There is nothing inherently wrong in this; in fact, small group relationships are usually encouraged for their benefits in mutual authenticity and accountability. However, when these social sub-groups become exclusive, shutting out other people, the inclusive grace of God may be contradicted by the actions of those involved in such groups (Eph. 2:11–13), and the unity of the Body of Christ may be jeopardized (Eph. 2:14–18). Exclusive groups often find themselves in competition with or mistrustful of other, similarly exclusive groups, and unhealthy political dynamics come into play as a result. It is difficult for any leader to gain and maintain trust in such circumstances.

Behaviors relating to decision-making processes

Several questions in the Trust Scale pertain to decision-making processes. Playing politics (question 11), making "decisions affecting others without involving others" (question 16), springing surprises on others (question 26), and ignoring input from others (question 27) are behaviors that breed mistrust.[66]

---

64. Covey, *Speed of Trust*.
65. Guder, *Missional Church*.
66. Hultman, *Making Change Irresistible*.

Political maneuvering drains energy and attention away from an organization's ability to fulfill its vision.[67] When politics rule the functioning of an organization, people become very self-protective and suspicious of everyone else who is not aligned with their views.[68] Just like business and non-profit organizations, many congregations have their "power brokers," "turf lords," and others who wield their own influence or seek to align themselves with those who do hold power in order to advance their own agenda. This is particularly dangerous when that agenda is in conflict with the church's values and norms.[69] The key to building trust in churches is in forming strong, collaborative ministry teams that are focused on fulfilling the mission and vision of the Church and which model the values and norms that the Church embraces.[70]

When decisions need to be made in any organization, it is imperative to involve everyone affected by the decision in the decision-making process.[71] When some people are not included in the process, they may feel that decisions are being imposed upon them and they fear that they are thus losing control over their life circumstances.[72] The principle of including others in decision-making is found in the Scriptures. When the first-century church was wrestling with the issue of the place of Gentiles in the Church, they first listened to all the groups involved, and then Peter addressed the entire group. They also gave opportunity to Paul and Barnabas to address the group, telling what God had been doing among the Gentiles (Acts 15:6–7). The process the early Church followed enabled a serious issue to be addressed while maintaining the unity of the Church. Unfortunately, many churches in the early twenty-first century do not follow the example of the first-century Church but engage in negative behaviors that produce a culture of mistrust, which leads to resistance to even the most godly change proposal.

The springing of surprises on others (question 26) can have a negative effect on trust within a congregation. Decisions that are seen as reactions to the latest crisis may not inspire confidence in most congregants. Most members want some advance notice of changes that are being proposed

67. Lencioni, *Five Dysfuctions*.
68. Kotter and Cohen, *Heart of Change*.
69. Covey, *Speed of Trust*.
70. Lewis and Cordeiro, *Culture Shift*.
71. Lines et al., "Production of Trust."
72. Oreg, "Resistance to Change."

and an opportunity to give input in the decision-making process.[73] There may be more readiness to change when changes are planned in advance in alignment with the mission and vision of the church and people "are provided with information about the imminence of change and the likely duration of change."[74]

When changes are implemented without giving opportunity for input, resistance to those changes may be the result, as there is no "mutuality of influence."[75] Some people interpret this behavior as a lack of respect on the part of the leaders toward the followers.[76] Instead of ignoring the input of others, leaders need to listen carefully to what people tell them, because this gives people confidence that "their interests and values are understood and taken seriously."[77] This advice assumes, of course, that those to whom one is listening have earned the right to be heard by their own mature attitude and healthy behavior. Rewarding unhealthy actions by granting a privileged audience will likely only encourage such behavior in the future. As in many other relational dynamics, this is an area in which deep discernment is necessary.

Behaviors promoting self-interests over corporate interests

Some of the questions in the Trust Scale pertain to seeking one's own interests over corporate interests such as "seek win-lose outcomes" (question 13), "look out for their own interests" (question 14), "have a we-they mentality" (question 23), and "undercut others" (question 9). It was noted earlier in this chapter that people may often resist change if they do not see how a change will personally benefit them.[78] These kinds of self-serving behaviors are so contrary to the Spirit of Christ, who did not come to this earth seeking his own benefit, but he came for the sake of others. Paul said to the Corinthians, "Nobody should seek his own good, but the good of others" (1 Cor. 10:24, NIV), and told the Galatians that the whole Law is "summed up in a single command, 'Love your neighbor as yourself'" (Gal.

---

73. Kanter, "Enduring Skills."
74. Rafferty and Griffin, "Perceptions of Organizational Change," 1155.
75. Lines et al., "Production of Trust," 225.
76. Lawrence, "Resistance to Change," 8.
77. Lines et al., "Production of Trust," 239. See also Anderson and Anderson, "Critical Mass," and Lawrence, "Resistance to Change."
78. Rafferty and Griffin, "Perceptions of Organizational Change," and Wanberg and Banas, "Predictors and Outcomes."

5:14, NIV). Followers of Christ should not take advantage of the vulnerability of others by making decisions that benefit self at the expense of others, which happens when win-lose outcomes are sought.[79]

The undercutting of others is pushing personal agendas at the expense of others; tearing others down in order to move ahead of them. Paul told the Corinthians that God had given him authority for "building [them] up and not for tearing [them] down" (2 Cor. 13:10, NIV). Edification is at the root of what it means to be a member of a church: building others up, supporting others, doing everything possible to help others reach their goals and fulfill their responsibilities. When these behaviors are done voluntarily, they help to build a culture of trust.[80]

The seeking of one's own interests is sometimes manifested in hidden agendas (question 19), competitiveness (question 20), manipulative tactics (question 15), and the use of information for one's own advantage (question 29). Paul insisted that he did not have any hidden agendas. He was not trying to mislead the Corinthians regarding his plans to visit them and asked them, "Do I make my plans in a worldly manner so that in the same breath I say 'Yes, yes' and 'No, no?'" (2 Cor. 1:17, NIV). When accused of being in competition with other apostles, Paul responded, "The man who plants and the man who waters have one purpose, and each will be rewarded according to his own labor. For we are God's fellow-workers" (1 Cor. 3:8–9, NIV). When his motives were questioned, Paul responded, "I am not writing this to shame you, but to warn you as my dear children" (1 Cor. 4:14, NIV).

Sometimes the seeking of one's own interests involves the intimidation of others. Some organizations are known for their cultures of domination, which seek to advance the interests of one group over another through exploitation and control.[81] The Bible warns leaders against "lording it over the flock" which occurs when a leader is seeking to force his or her will and interests over the congregation (1 Peter 5:2). Paul wanted the Corinthians to know that he was not trying to intimidate them with his epistles when he wrote, "I do not want to seem to be trying to frighten you with my letters" (2 Cor. 10:9, NIV).

---

79. Lines et al., "Production of Trust."
80. Ferrin et al., "Interpersonal Trust."
81. Michael Chase, personal communication, 12 February 2007.

Behaviors involving active aggression

As noted in the previous chapter, behavioral resistance is one of the dimensions of resistance that is difficult for congregational leaders and congregants alike to ignore. Sometimes resistance goes beyond strong emotion to aggressive action. We on occasion have had ministry colleagues involve the police in order to protect themselves from individuals who were behaving in a very threatening, hostile manner in a church office or worship service. And we have seen or heard of situations in which a pastor or church leader was the one behaving aggressively. Power is almost always a difficult thing to hold, and those who hold it with anger will almost always misuse it.

Question 24 asks about the prevalence of open attacks within the congregation and question 21 asks about revenge or the attempts to get even with others. When these types of actions are occurring within a congregation, other people naturally move into a defensive posture, which does nothing to build trust. When we do not feel safe, we will not take additional risks. Therefore, unsafe or aggressive behavior must be addressed decisively and quickly, with deference given first and foremost to matters of safety and then to biblical principles of Christian community. Paul wrote to the Colossians that they were to "bear with each other and forgive whatever grievances you may have against one another" (Col. 3:13, NIV) and to the Thessalonians to "make sure that no one pays back wrong for wrong, but always try to be kind to each other and to everyone else" (1 Thess. 5:15, NIV). To the Romans he wrote, "If it is possible, as far as it depends on you, live at peace with everyone. Do not take revenge" (Rom. 12:18–19, NIV). Those who cannot covenant to live at peace with others may need to be loved from a distance, until they demonstrate their trustworthiness for more intimate relationships.

WHY THIS MATTERS

What has been shown in this examination of the questions of Hultman's Trust Scale is that, while it asks questions about the prevalence of negative behaviors in the congregation and these are contrary to the Spirit of Christ, there are contrasting positive behaviors that foster trust stipulated in the Bible.[82] It is not enough for a congregation to merely talk about trust

---

82. For a chart summarizing the positive behaviors that build trust, please go to the companion website for this book at www.leadingmissionalchange.info

issues but the members need to focus on practicing behaviors that build trust. While some may be prone to condemn the actions and behaviors that foster mistrust, especially as they have been shown to be contrary to the principles of the Bible and contrary to the Spirit of Christ, it is far more important to concentrate on living the behaviors that will build trust in one another.

In these past couple of chapters we have explored the various dimensions of resistance to change and the qualities needed for a readiness to embrace missional change. We have uncovered recent research on the dynamics of change leadership that demonstrates, again and again, that it is far more important for a leader to foster a culture within an organization that is creative, flexible, and permeated thoroughly with an atmosphere of trust, rather than to simply react against those who initially resist change initiatives. Such a culture may be transformative, enabling many within the organization to become initiators and embracers of change. Thus, when opportunities present themselves for significant ministry to the unchurched or for a fresh encounter with God among those who already follow Jesus, a church that is ready to change can be out in the forefront, ready to seize those opportunities, ready to experiment, ready to try any legitimate means to live out the kingdom of God. In the following chapters we summarize how we sought to confirm this through research with real congregations, and what we learned from that about the readiness of churches to embrace missional change. But, first, Tony will share his "tale of two churches" about his own experience in both successfully and unsuccessfully leading missional change.

5

Tony's Story

A Tale of Two Churches

"Prophesy to these bones and say to them, 'Dry bones, hear the word of the LORD! This is what the Sovereign LORD says to these bones: I will make breath enter you, and you will come to life. I will attach tendons to you and make flesh come upon you and cover you with skin; I will put breath in you, and you will come to life. Then you will know that I am the LORD'"

(EZEKIEL 37:4–6)

IT WAS THE WORST OF TIMES

THE SANCTUARY WAS FULL on Sunday mornings. So were the classrooms and the parking lot. For me, a young, "up-and-coming" pastor of a medium-sized suburban congregation, this was both satisfying and troubling. It was satisfying in that the ministries we had put in place were obviously meeting the needs of people in the community and the congregation's reputation was strong. More and more people were seeking us out and, it was obvious, were seeking the Lord and not just snazzy programs. It was also satisfying on a personal level, for I had been sent to this congregation to be senior pastor at age 26, far too young in retrospect, but I had something to prove. My predecessor, who was only a few years older than I, had been well loved in this congregation and had started them on a track toward growth. I was expected to continue that pattern. And, now, three years into that role, with attendance at Sunday morning worship services rising each year, I was finally feeling a bit secure in my own leadership abilities and in the long-term prospects for this ministry. Particularly if the people kept on coming.

But if there were no space for them, new people would quit. The committed folks would put up with it, for sure, but visitors would likely go elsewhere rather than be stuffed up against strangers. And that was beginning to happen. So I proposed what seemed to be a reasonable solution: that we start a second worship service on Sunday mornings to accommodate the larger numbers that God seemed to be sending our way. Many, many churches have multiple worship services and, while they require additional labor to staff them, I was willing to preach twice on Sundays, and I suspected that we would have enough volunteers to make a good effort at it. Besides, we already had fully-staffed children's programs during both the Sunday School hour and the worship hour. I proposed that we keep those as they were, split the adult Sunday School classes between the two services, and simply add a worship service in the sanctuary during the Sunday School hour. If we found that it was going well, we could eventually use it to start a daughter church in another part of our town (a goal first articulated by my predecessor that I had warmly embraced).

Soon thereafter my family and I left for a week's vacation. When we returned, I was summoned to a meeting of the Personnel Relations Commission, which informed me that the deacons had met during my absence and were asking for my resignation. A second service sounded too much like a church split to them, and in their fear they had decided to get rid of the one they perceived as causing the problem. Besides, some admitted that they weren't too sure that they wanted all these new people in their church. They were distressed that their pastor was spending so much time and energy caring for the newcomers and felt that the old-timers were being neglected. Besides, they said, "we want someone with stronger leadership skills."

Oh my! I had not seen this one coming, not at all. I had had a decade of experience as a pastor by this point, and every church had grown. People had come to know Jesus as their Savior and believers had grown deeper in their spiritual journey. I had started successful new programs, improved communications, hired staff, and made other changes that were generally approved of and appreciated. No, the problem was the second service proposal, and in my relative youth and "go-full-steam" attitude I had missed something very important. This church had split several years before; a previous pastor had taken a sizable portion of the congregation and started his own church just a few miles down the road. For the survivors of that, a second service felt very much like the same thing. It meant that longtime friends might worship at separate times, and that relationships might suffer because people might not even pass each other in the hallway. Yes, those are some of the challenges of multiple worship services and, yes, they can be addressed. But I was not hearing their fears and concerns, and so missed the early signals.

Daniel Goleman is the guru of "emotional intelligence" and has written a book by that name. I was pretty sharp with my intellectual intelligence and even organizational intelligence, but if I had known about emotional intelligence at the time and had paid attention to those relational dynamics, I would have done things differently. We might have gotten our second worship service implemented, but I would have moved more slowly and had more conversations and listened more closely and perhaps incorporated aspects into the proposal that would have better addressed these concerns. And I'm sure I could have created a more hospitable environment for feedback, else they would not have felt the need to dismiss me while I was out of town. That was a particularly cowardly act, to be sure, and revealed much about their character. But it also told me that they had not perceived me as open to changing my mind.

In this situation, I had followed a standard model of change leadership, later articulated by John Kotter of Harvard Business School in his book *Leading Change*. I have heard many pastors swear by Kotter and his eight-step linear method of leading change in organizations. He argues that a leader must create a vision for change in order to solve a problem in an organization. To do so, that leader creates a coalition of influential people to help "sell" the change to others. If successful, change is implemented, everyone is happy, and the leader is praised. If unsuccessful, the people conclude that either the leader's vision is flawed or the leader is ineffective in persuading people to change. Many pastors who have attempted significant missional change in their churches and have been stymied have been so labeled. And, worse, many of them have believed the label, and have concluded that they are ineffective leaders or were not truly called to pastoral ministry to begin with. Too many have dropped out of ministry because they hit a wall of congregational resistance and internalized the resultant criticism.

Maybe the model is wrong. I have since discovered another approach to leading change, one pioneered by David Cooperrider of Case Western Reserve University. It's called "appreciative inquiry"[1] and it consists of a process of asking questions of the members of an organization or community. It begins with listening, not talking. The questions are focused on what works well, instead of what problems need to be solved. And from that process of inquiry stories and symbols begin to emerge, along with ideas and solutions and ideals that the community wishes to embrace. Leaders can then articulate back to the community what they have heard and lead their people to accomplish the things they already wish to do and become. It's a much more bottom-up, people-centric, solution-focused approach to leading change than the Kotter model. I have found in the years since that it is both more effective and more affirming of those of whom change is asked.

IT WAS THE BEST OF TIMES

Little did I know when I was packing my bags after being fired that I would soon have the opportunity to practice a form of appreciative inquiry, although I had never heard of the term or concept at that point. I was devastated by the church's decision to fire me and actually feared that my pastoral career was over. I did not have the emotional strength to start all over with a new ministry at that point, I was sure, and was hoping to eventually pursue an academic career anyway, so I started applying to local colleges and universities for teaching opportunities. I was given one that Fall, a temporary three-quarter-time position that provided a measure of financial security for my family and some free time for other things. That free time was soon filled by an interim assignment, expected to last three months or so, at a very small, rural congregation in a nearby county. The church was in significant decline and there were questions about whether it would survive. I was asked by the conference to work part-time for them, doing some preaching and some limited pastoral care, and in the process to assess its long-term potential.

Those three months lasted six years, as that interim assignment become one of the most delightful experiences in my ministry career. The

---

1 . Cooperrider and Whitney, *Appreciative Inquiry*.

church did not close; rather, we experienced a renewal that resulted in a fresh approach to that community, including the creation of a community care center. We built an addition to our building, hired additional staff, started a second worship service (yes, I finally got that, but at another church!), and experienced the grace of God in a way that was new and restorative to all of us. How did that happen?

When I arrived at Strinestown (the name of the church and the community), I was bleeding emotionally. I had just been dismissed from my previous charge, I didn't know how I was going to feed my family beyond the current semester, and I had been branded a "failure" by those I had attempted to lead. So in my despair I latched onto a song by Christian recording artist Steve Taylor. It was called "Jesus is for Losers," and its tongue-in-cheek message was that Jesus had a special affection for all the losers of the world. I felt like one . . . but so did my congregation, I was soon to discover. They, too, felt like they had failed, that their once-vibrant church was but a shadow of itself. And many felt like losers in their personal lives as well, for they were dealing with all the normal stuff of life. When I looked closer, I discovered that many people in our community felt like losers too; once a comfortable middle-class community, it had transitioned into a rural "welfare community," with many of the houses rented to short-term tenants and mobile home parks on both ends of town. Many of our neighbors had moved here to hide or had secrets they didn't want to share.

So we adopted "Jesus is for Losers" as our church slogan. Yes, we even put it on the church sign out front. I heard brakes squeal as people drove by and saw that sign. And it generated lots of questions . . . which, of course, was the point. And we got to explain, again and again, that Jesus has a special affection for all who feel like they're losers, for all who have screwed up and need a second chance, all who have been rejected, pushed aside, or marginalized, all who are getting what they "deserve" but have genuine regrets about their past choices, all who simply have lost out in the luck of the draw. We went to the prophets, to the beatitudes, to the glory of grace itself . . . a word that had new, wonderful meaning for me personally!...and discovered afresh what our Gospel was all about.

And then we began to practice that grace in our neighborhood. We went door to door giving away fresh loaves of bread. We sponsored car washes and other random acts of kindness just to serve our neighbors . . . and refused their offered donations. We canceled a poorly-attended Sunday evening worship service that was essentially a retread of Sunday morning anyway, and instead erected a volleyball net in the yard and invited anyone who wanted to come play. We got to know them, and they got to know us. Relationships were created and trust was built, and when they were ready to risk walking inside the building or simply sharing their stories with us, we were prepared to receive that gift and honor them for it. People met Jesus in some wonderfully transformative ways and told their stories to others, who also began to suspect that perhaps something good was going on down at the church.

All of that did not happen overnight, of course. It required an internal transformation on my part, as I glimpsed more and more of the grace of God calling me out of my pain and into his goodness. And it required the members of the congregation to trust me as I encouraged them out of old patterns and into new expressions of their faith, particularly in their relationships with those outside our walls. That did not come automatically, but with each new success or each new face in worship, they grew in their confidence in me as leader and, more importantly, in the continuing love of God for them and their church. A decisive moment in that journey was a "Double Day" we attempted sometime during that first year. On that day, our goal was to double our usual attendance and offering. Realizing how critical that event was, I worked overtime inviting pretty much everyone I knew and gave a hefty donation besides. But, as it turned out, I wasn't the only one. They believed that this was possible and so they were doing the same. When Double Day came, we discovered that we had exceeded our goals. More importantly, we believed that other, more stretching goals were possible for us.

That positive change experience grew out of a relational connection between me and the members of that congregation. They knew I was hurting. They knew I had just come from a larger, more vibrant ministry. I didn't have the emotional energy to try to pretend with them; rather, I chose authenticity and lived out my journey of grace and trust in front of them. And I relaxed, for I wasn't planning on a long-term ministry. I didn't feel that I had anything to prove to them. I was just going to be there for a while and leave. But that authenticity engendered relational connection. When, at the end of my original three months, they asked me to stay on, the lay leader noted that I "fit like an old shoe." It was a compliment.

THE POWER OF TRUST

I learned a lot about leadership, both positive and negative, in these two churches. The first church taught me the power of organization and programming to attract new people to something that was growing and vibrant, but it also revealed the weaknesses of changes that are initiated entirely at the leadership level and not bought into by the congregation. I still believe that what I was proposing was the right thing to do . . . but wish very much I had done it a different way. When I got to Strinestown, I had learned the hard way that such efforts are not always embraced. In that atmosphere of uncertainty and ambiguity, a deep relational connection opened up possibilities for leader, congregation, and community that none of us would have uncovered on our own, that never would have emerged had we not engaged in an intentional process of listening to each other, honoring each other, and, over time, trusting each other.

Paul and I have heard countless stories since, in my own subsequent leadership opportunities and in the accounts of others, that reinforce these general principles. As we compared our own stories and even walked with each other through them at certain stages of the journey, we discovered the similarities. And as we listened to and observed others, we began to note these same patterns. We saw pastor after pastor frustrated by churches that "simply won't change" or earnest laypersons distressed that their pastors "won't lead," or denominational leaders stymied by congregations that seemed to "lack vision for their community." And so Paul engaged in a research study, with a little bit of guidance from me, to determine if what we were seeing and experiencing was common, and to better understand the unique dynamics at work. Was it possible to diagnose what churches were more open to change than others? Was it possible to identify certain critical factors that would help a pastor or visionary layperson lead a positive change effort? The following chapters explain that effort and what we learned.

6

A Little Research Project

Trust and Mission in Real Congregations

WHAT'S REALLY GOING ON OUT THERE?

THE SOURCES WE'VE REVIEWED have shown that a key factor in congregational readiness to implement missional change is trust. It appears that mistrust may hamper missional change initiatives while a culture of trust provides an environment where people might be more open to change and may find change irresistible. When resistance related to mistrust is recognized and addressed and readiness to change is inculcated into the very fabric of the congregation through behaviors that build trust, proposed missional changes may be accepted and implemented. Both of these factors are essential, but the lack of resistance doesn't necessarily mean that people are open to change.

But at this point we've had only a theory. What's really going on out there in the churches? Intuitively, it seems right that trust levels would affect a congregation's resistance or readiness to change, but can we prove it? Or at least find a sufficient correlation to cause us to look more closely at how we can better build trust in leadership situations? That's the reason for this chapter. Surprisingly, little formal research has addressed the extent of trust and mistrust within congregations or determined if trust or mistrust have any impact upon congregational resistance or readiness to change. So we designed our own research study, the intent of which was to diagnose the levels of trust and mistrust within participating congregations and to analyze growth trends within those congregations to determine if there is a correlation between trust and readiness for missional change.

As one might expect, Hultman's Trust Scale was the instrument chosen for the diagnosis of trust and mistrust, and congregations belonging to the U.S. National Conference of the Church of the United Brethren in Christ were invited to participate in the project. Attendance and conversion records for a ten-year period were obtained from this denomination to analyze congregational growth or decline patterns, which were compared to the congregational "trust score" from the survey. Many of the participating pastors provided us with anecdotal data regarding missional change initiatives in their local congregations, making possible a clearer connection between trust, missional change, and congregational growth.

SOME FAIRLY NORMAL U.S. CHURCHES

The Church of the United Brethren in Christ (UBIC) was chosen for a study of the impact of trust and mistrust on readiness for missional change. The decision to research this particular denomination was made, not only because it is the judicatory body holding both of our ordination credentials, but also because it has a well established historical pattern of resistance to change initiatives. The UBIC denomination retains, without modification, its original Statement of Faith, initially drafted in 1789 and adopted in 1815. The UBIC denomination also retains, with only minor modifications, its original Constitution adopted in 1841. The denomination suffered a devastating split in the 1880s due to attempts to change the constitution, and recent attempts to introduce missional change on a denomination-wide basis have met with mixed reactions.

Now, we love the UBIC movement for several reasons, not least of which is that it has maintained, with some difficulty, a "broadly evangelical" witness in an era in which minor doctrinal differences have repeatedly divided or erected barriers between Christian groups. Their statement of faith is bold but brief, so the United Brethren can embrace brothers and sisters who disagree with each other on matters that would divide others but remain united in our confession that Jesus is Lord. But the personal stories we have shared in previous chapters are of our experiences in United Brethren churches, and they are not at all atypical. We know the challenges of serving in a movement that has experienced a marvelous work of the Holy Spirit and then ossified in that for decades. Sadly, this is fairly normal among U.S. churches. So we thought that if any group could reveal patterns of resistance to missional change, our UBIC brothers and sisters might prove to be a helpful laboratory.

In the latter part of the twentieth century, the UBIC showed signs on a national or international level of being more open to change and willing to explore new denominational structures and ministry models, as detailed in chapter one. However, this denominational readiness to change has not filtered down to the local church level and, from our experience (and that of many of our colleagues), resistance to change appears to be prevalent in U.S. UBIC churches. This bifurcation of goals has created a significant amount of the frustration that we have observed among pastors: many wish to lead congregations in a missional manner and are encouraged by their own leaders to do so, but experience significant resistance to this at the local level. Because of the desire of U.S. national leaders to see churches overcoming resistance to change, it seemed appropriate to approach the U.S. National Bishop for authorization to study the issue of trust and mistrust in hopes of shedding light on the roots of this problem in the churches. The Bishop gave his approval to the study, and a survey of the UBIC churches was conducted soon thereafter.

A random sampling of the 221 United Brethren in Christ churches across the United States comprised the participants of this study. Some were eliminated because they had not reported sufficient attendance and conversion data to complete a longitudinal study (a study over time). The UBICs are, like most evangelical denominations, comprised primarily of small or medium-sized churches. For the purposes of classification, we designated 108 of the sample churches as "small," averaging less than 100 in attendance; forty-five were "medium-sized" churches, averaging between 100 and 250 in attendance; and seventeen were "large," averaging over 250 in attendance. Therefore, a total of 170 churches across the United States were available to contact for a survey on the prevalence of congregational trust and mistrust. And then a random sample of thirty was chosen for the full survey. Thirty churches represent fourteen percent of all of the congregations in the United States. It was anticipated that this number of churches would provide statistically significant data for this project.

Invitations to participate in the survey were sent to UBIC pastors. Selected church addresses were obtained from the UBIC website church directory (www.ub.org) and entered into a database built for the analysis of the survey results. If a pastor listed an e-mail address in the church directory, we electronically sent the pastor an invitation to participate in the trust survey. If no e-mail address was available, the invitation to participate was sent by mail to the pastor. We anticipated that this selection method would give us a good range of differences in UBIC congregations in church size, locality, and ethnicity. While many of these churches are largely comprised of Caucasian, non-Hispanic congregants, an increasing number of churches cater to a particular ethnic population, including Hispanics, African-Americans, and Chinese. It was anticipated that the geographical region and ethnicity of the congregation would not have any significant impact on the results of the survey.

MEASURING TRUST

The instrument used for this research was a modification of Hultman's Trust Scale, which we introduced earlier. The "Trust Scale" is a non-standardized survey that has been used in non- profit and business settings, but to the best of our knowledge, the survey had never been used in a congregational setting. The purpose of the survey, which consists of thirty statements pertaining to behaviors that contribute to mistrust, is to assess the degree to which those behaviors are present in a team or group. Our biblical survey demonstrated that the behaviors tracked in the Trust Scale have great relevance for a congregational setting because those behaviors are contrary to the Spirit of Christ and are violations of biblical principles of conduct. However, because the "Trust Scale" was designed for business and non-profit organizations, two words were changed on Hultman's tool to make his instrument specifically applicable to a congregational setting. While the original Trust Scale prefaces each of the thirty statements with the phrase, "The people on my team," the congregational survey uses the phrase, "The people in my congregation." The modified inventory is included in appendix A.

The behaviors addressed in Hultman's Trust Scale include many different types. A number of behaviors involve breakdowns in communication (e.g., gossip, withholding information, and inconsistent messaging). Other behaviors relate to reactions to errors (e.g., blaming others and making excuses), while other behaviors have to do with the provision of feedback (e.g., criticism and put downs). Some behaviors involve building exclusivist cultures (e.g., formation of cliques), while others revolve around corporate decision-making (e.g., political maneuvering, unilateral decisions, and springing surprises). Most damaging are behaviors that promote self-interest over corporate interests (e.g., seeking win-lose outcomes and undercutting others) and active aggression (e.g., attacking others and seeking revenge).

When the targeted negative behaviors are present within a congregation, they contribute to an atmosphere of mistrust, which results in resistance to change. However, it is not enough for a congregation to just avoid the negative behaviors to build a culture of trust. The use of the Trust Scale verifies the presence or absence of the negative behaviors that breed mistrust. Further research is needed to determine the impact of positive behaviors on building a culture of trust within congregations.

Adult members of the participating congregations were given a copy of the Trust Scale with instructions to complete the survey based only upon what had actually been observed within the congregation and not what people may have perceived to be present. Each participating adult was instructed to evaluate how frequently he or she had observed each of the thirty behaviors addressed on the survey. If a particular behavior had almost never been observed in the interpersonal relationships within the congregation, he or she was to rank that behavior as a "4" and a behavior had almost always seen that behavior, he or she was to rank that behavior as a "0." Mid-rankings of frequently, occasionally, or rarely could be given a score of "1," "2," or "3" respectively. The completed surveys were returned to us for tabulation and analysis. A low score on this instrument indicated a high level of mistrust within the organization while a high score indicated a high level of trust. By placing these thirty statements in rank order, the behaviors that most contribute to mistrust within a congregation were identified.

The pastors willing to participate in the survey were either mailed a packet with the number of surveys requested and a postage-paid envelope for return mail, or directed to an online version of the survey created for this purpose. A short questionnaire (see appendix B) was included for the pastor to complete to provide some additional information of missional change initiatives in the church and community. Completed surveys were collected by the pastor or designated member and returned to us for analysis. For analytical purposes, it was desired that between ten and twenty percent of the adult members or attendees of a congregation would return a completed instrument. It was understood that this would be difficult to achieve in some of the congregations because many of the churches were very small. Some of the participating congregations were too small for valid congregational statistical analysis to be done, but their responses were included with the overall survey results.

For those churches with sufficient responses, the results were sent to the pastors. In addition to the overall score and frequency table, the pastors received a list of all the survey questions in ranked order from highest score to lowest score for that particular congregation. The ranked list enabled the pastors to see the behaviors most contributing to trust and the behaviors most contributing to mistrust within that individual congregation only. We compared the overall "trust score" with the demographic and anecdotal data to determine if there may be a linkage between the degree of trust in a congregation and the success or failure of attempts to implement missional change.

Upon the conclusion of the survey process, we tallied all of the responses together to ascertain denominational norms and median scores. This provided a benchmark for the participating churches to see how they scored in relation to the entire survey population. A final report showing the overall scores and the five behaviors most contributing to trust and mistrust in the churches was provided to the Bishop and to the participating pastors.[1]

In order to find correlations between the trust scores, missional orientation, and resistance to or readiness for change, post-research congregational case studies were conducted. You can read some of them in chapter 7. The churches so studied were small churches with varying missional orientations. The pastors of those congregations had completed the follow-up questionnaire, which provided ample information and examples of resistance to and readiness for missional change.

MEASURING MISSION

An important aspect of this project was seeking to determine how the level of trust in a congregation would impact its readiness to implement missional change. The Congregational Trust Survey was a critical tool in verifying the presence or absence of the behaviors contributing to mistrust

1. For a downloadable copy of the final report, please go to the companion website for this book at www.leadingmissionalchange.info

within a fellowship of believers. It was necessary to take another step to see how that level of trust would enable or hinder the fulfillment of God's mission and purpose for the local church. We went looking for a way to assess the missional orientation of local congregations. We also explored, through responses to the pastors' questionnaires and other contacts with UBIC pastors, the ways that trust has impacted congregational readiness or resistance to change.

The missional orientation of a congregation is the determination of whether or not a church is in an outwardly focused missional mode or an inwardly focused maintenance mode. But assessing the missional orientation of a congregation from a distance is not an easy task for a researcher. So many factors could impact the ability of a congregation to fulfill the mission God has given, such as the spiritual openness of the surrounding culture, the giftedness of a congregation and its leaders, and the frequency of pastoral transitions. Another factor that cannot be measured from a distance is the involvement of the membership in mission outside of the congregation. For example, the involvement of members in community organizations could provide opportunities for building relationships with unchurched neighbors and these developing relationships could open up opportunities for spiritual conversations to take place. The number of members who have conversations of a spiritual nature with unchurched friends and neighbors and the frequency of those conversations would be a better indicator of the missional orientation of a congregation than looking at attendance and conversion statistics alone.

Nevertheless, attendance, conversion, membership, and baptismal records of denominational congregations can provide indicators of missional orientation. When members are in a growing relationship with Christ and are finding spiritual nourishment and encouragement through their involvement in the local church, they are likely to invite others to come with them to experience the same spiritual benefits, which may result in higher average attendance. When the members are engaged in spiritual conversations with unchurched friends and neighbors, there is likely to be an increase in the number of conversions recorded in the local church. When a church is actively engaged in discipleship and training of new believers, there is likely to be an increase in the number of people submitting to the rite of baptism and committing themselves to the responsibilities of membership in the local church. Therefore, congregational statistics may be a reasonable indicator of a church's missional orientation.

A Little Research Project

Fortunately, UBIC churches are required to file an annual report, and that data proved to be very helpful in completing our research. We recognize that self-reporting has some limitations or cautions but these were minimized by the fact that we were less interested in the data reported by any church in any given year, for instance, and more interested in how those self-reported numbers changed over time. Congregational attendance, conversion, baptism, and membership records from annual reports provided to the denominational headquarters were analyzed to estimate the missional orientation of the denomination and its congregations. The analysis of the data took into consideration the size of the congregations, and calculated the factors of missional orientation based upon averages of comparably sized churches. Some fluctuations between categories occurred in several churches over the ten-year period, a reason why we decided to utilize the ten-year average weekly attendance as the defining point for church size designations.

It must be noted that missional orientation is not dependent upon the size of a congregation. A church may be small in comparison to others, but it may still be fulfilling the purpose for which God has designed it. A church may be medium or large, but there may be other factors that hinder it from fulfilling God's purpose, and therefore such a church could be in a maintenance mode instead of a missional mode. Therefore, it was essential to find other means of comparison to objectively ascertain whether or not the congregational statistics would indicate missional orientation.

Five factors not dependent upon church size were used in the calculation of the missional orientation of congregations. The first factor that was true of all congregations, regardless of church size, was the number of years in which a congregation experienced growth. If the average weekly attendance was greater than the average weekly attendance in a prior year, growth had occurred. The number of years in which the congregation experienced growth was used in the calculation of missional orientation. The same type of calculation was used for membership growth. Annual growth rates were calculated for the ten-year period for each of the denominational churches, and the number of years in which congregations attained a growth rate of five percent a year or better was totaled and used in the missional orientation calculation.

The number of annual conversions recorded by local churches varies widely between churches of different sizes, so a means of comparison that was not dependent upon church size was needed for this data. The average number of annual conversions was calculated for large, medium, and small churches, and the number of years a congregation recorded a number greater than the average annual conversions for its size was totaled and used in the calculation of missional orientation. The same kind of calculation was used for baptisms performed. Notice that neither we nor the denomination's annual report asked the pastors to define what they meant by "conversion." However defined by a particular leader or congregation, our interest was the pattern established over the previous decade.

The five factors of the number of years a church experienced growth, attained a growth rate of five percent or better, increased the membership roll, and recorded conversion rates and baptisms greater than national averages of churches of comparable size gave us an objective and reasonable means of assessing the long-term missional orientation of UBIC congregations. It should be noted, however, that a congregation's missional orientation might change over a period of time. Strong missional congregations may shift into a maintenance mode, while churches in maintenance mode may be transformed missionally.

The five factors for each congregation were totaled to produce what was called a "missional quotient" (MQ), and this score was compared to the trust score of the participating congregations to determine if a correlation existed between an atmosphere of trust and a missional orientation. The assumption that congregations that had a strong missional orientation would be most ready for missional change was a given. The overall "trust score" for each church was compared to the decadal and one-year growth rates to determine if there was any correlation between levels of trust and congregational growth or decline. The trust score was also cross-checked against the MQ of the congregation to determine if trust was higher in congregations with a missional orientation. The anecdotal information provided by the participating pastors was also examined to find any linkage between readiness for missional change initiatives and levels of trust within the congregation.

We were working under the assumption that congregations with a high readiness for missional change may be more likely to experience conversion growth. Congregations with an outward focus may be more likely to attract and influence individuals within the surrounding culture to make faith commitments. They may look for opportunities to reach out to those around them to share the Good News, which may result in increased participation within the life of the congregation. We wanted to determine if resistance to missional change in declining churches may be the result of high levels of mistrust. If this proved to be the case, pastors would need to give greater attention to those behaviors that build trust within the congregation before embarking on any attempts to implement missional change. Building a culture of trust in the church may be the key to turning around a congregation and moving it into a period of growth. On the other hand, we also wanted to see if readiness to accept missional change in churches beginning to experience growth may result from high levels of trust. If this proved to be the case, pastors would need to zealously guard against any of the behaviors that would undermine trust in their own lives and within the life of the congregation, so that resistance might not replace the readiness for missional change.

We've explained our research process in some detail here for two reasons. There's much more we could say, about coding and other matters, but we wanted to give you enough detail so you could have confidence in the results we reveal and discuss here. The quality of data is entirely dependent on the quality of the research process. The second reason is that we suggest that this process may be helpful to your own congregation. You can contact us to do for you what we did for the congregations in this study, or you can attempt it on your own. Either way, there may be something worth learning here about how much trust exists in your congregation (and in what ways it manifests), how your church compares in terms of missional orientation, and what linkage there may be between them.

WHAT WE FOUND: DENOMINATIONAL PATTERNS

Our analysis of annual reports of UBIC churches submitted to U.S. National Conference headquarters revealed that the U.S. National Conference was in a period of stagnation or slow decline. While the overall average attendance at Sunday morning services increased, the statistics revealed that during the decade more congregations experienced a decline than an increase. Most of the growth occurred in the larger churches. The records also showed that conversions did not translate into worship attendance, as there were 3.5 times as many recorded conversions as there were additional attendees in worship during that ten-year period. Because there was no quantifiable connection between the missional orientation of a congregation and church growth or size, it was necessary to take a deeper dive into the data to find metrics that might indicate if a church was in a maintenance mode or a missional mode.

As noted earlier, five factors gave us an objective and reasonable means of assessing the missional orientation of U.S. UBIC congregations; the number of years a church (a) experienced growth; (b) attained a growth rate of five percent or better; (c) increased the membership roll; (d) recorded conversion rates greater than national averages of churches of comparable size; and (e) recorded baptismal rates greater than national averages of churches of comparable size. These five factors for each congregation were totaled to produce a "missional quotient" (MQ). The MQ was compared to the trust score of the participating congregations to determine if a correlation existed between an atmosphere of trust and missional orientation. The maximum MQ possible for each congregation was 47.

The large churches (with average weekly attendance over 250) had the overall highest missional quotients. Sixteen large churches had scores that ranged from 20 to 42, with a mean of 28. (One large church was excluded from the calculations because it was a church plant with only three years of history.) The 45 medium churches (with average weekly attendance between 100 and 250) had scores that ranged from 6 to 32, with a mean of 19. One hundred and six small churches (with average weekly attendance less than 100) had scores that ranged from 2 to 36, with a mean of 15. (Two small congregations were excluded from the calculations because they were church plants, too new to have a decade's worth of growth patterns, but the existence of new church plants among the UBICs, by itself, is evidence of at least some missional orientation, independent of the data gathered for this project.)

When all scores were calculated together, irrespective of church size, the mean score was 17, which allowed us to categorize the churches as "Strong Missional" (42–23), "Missional" (22–17), "Maintenance" (16–12), and "Strong Maintenance" (11–2). The distribution of the congregations shows a fair balance in the denomination between congregations in maintenance and missional mode, with more congregations in the middle categories than on either "strong" side. The fact that no large churches are found in maintenance mode reinforces the conclusion from the earlier study of attendance and conversion records that most of the growth in UBIC churches is occurring in the larger churches. (Again, we note that these categories are based on self-reported and self-defined data; it is entirely possible that a "conversion" in a larger church may be defined more broadly than in a

A Little Research Project

small church, where one has greater opportunity to observe the behavior of the convert and the staying power of the decision.)

WHAT WE FOUND: CONGREGATIONAL PATTERNS

The MQ categories were used in the analysis of the trust scores from the Congregational Trust survey. It was expected that churches with a high MQ were likely to have scored high on the Trust Scale, while churches with a low MQ were likely to have lower trust scores. If this hypothesis could be proven, there would be a quantifiable link between missional orientation and trust. A total of 31 congregations participated in the survey, providing us with 456 responses for the analysis. Though the invitations were sent randomly to pastors, the congregations that participated were a good representation of all four categories of missional orientation. Only two large churches participated in the Congregational Trust Survey; one with one online response and one with thirty responses. However, an adequate number of small and medium churches provided sufficient responses to test our assumptions. One hundred and seventy U. S. United Brethren in Christ congregations were eligible to participate in the Congregational Trust Survey and we attempted contact with 82% of them. In the end, 31 churches participated.

Twenty-one of the participating congregations were churches with average weekly attendance less than 100. The average weekly attendance for these churches was 63 during the 10 years researched. Of these twenty-one churches, 67% of them had sustained losses in attendance over the decade but 57% had experienced a gain in weekly attendance during the year the survey was administered. Five of these small churches had experienced a gain in attendance over the 10 years, but two of those five churches had experienced a loss in attendance in the year the survey was administered. Two of the participating small churches had neither grown nor declined during the decade prior to the survey. These 21 small churches collectively reported 914 conversions during the ten-year period studied and an overall growth rate of 7%. Twenty percent of them had an MQ of "Strong Missional," 35% were "Missional," 20% were "Maintenance," and 15% were "Strong Maintenance." Two of the churches did not have sufficient history to classify them in any category.

Eight of the participating congregations were medium in size, with average weekly attendance between 100 and 250. The average weekly attendance for these churches was 152 during the 10 years researched. Of these churches, 75% of them had sustained losses in attendance over the previous 10 years but half of those churches had experienced a gain in weekly attendance in the year the survey was administered. One of the churches had experienced a gain in attendance over the previous 10 years, more than doubling in size. One of the participating churches had neither grown nor declined during the decade prior to the survey. The eight medium-sized churches together reported 717 conversions during the ten-year period studied, but a decadal decline of 9%. Of the eight congregations participating in the trust survey, 12% were "Strong Missional," 38% were "Missional," 38% were "Maintenance," and 12% were "Strong Maintenance." It should be noted that the majority of churches were ranked in the middle levels rather than in the outer categories.

Only two large churches participated in the survey, one with one online response, after the pastor declined to participate because of the perceived negative nature of the survey. The other large church provided 30 responses, which was better than 10% of the average weekly attendance. However, in order for a better comparative analysis of the results from the churches, the results from the large churches were not compared to the results from the small or medium churches in the UBIC.

We were amazed to discover, upon the completion of the survey, that an almost perfect balance of churches with all four missional orientation categories was represented in the participating congregations: 20% were "strong missional," 28% "missional," 24% "maintenance," and 28% "strong maintenance." The representation of all categories of MQ is important for substantiating a link between trust and congregational readiness for change.

WHAT WE FOUND: THE SURPRISING LACK OF CORRELATION OF TRUST AND MISSION

Originally, we determined that scores on the Congregational Trust Survey between 0 and 30 indicated "Strong Mistrust," 31 to 60 indicated "Mistrust," 61 to 90 indicated "Trust," and 91 to 120 indicated "Strong Trust." But all 31 churches surveyed had Trust Scale scores above 60! And then the data got even weirder. An almost equal number of churches ranked missional and maintenance had equally high rankings in congregational trust Scores. On the surface, this seemed to disprove our hypothesis that churches with a strong missional orientation will have higher trust scores than churches

A Little Research Project

with a maintenance orientation. We were quite surprised by this, and it caused us to evaluate our assumptions a bit.

On the one hand, this could reflect a bias in the research design. It is possible that only churches with higher levels of trust would have been willing to participate in the survey. But it was still difficult at first to comprehend how missional congregations would have lower trust scores than maintenance congregations. But then we realized that the shift from "maintenance" to "missional" almost always involves conflict, and that conflict will often reduce trust levels. In other words, a lower level of trust might actually mean that something good is going on! And a higher level of trust might mean that a leader is well supported but has not capitalized on the trust of his or her people to lead them into a more missional orientation. This explanation is examined further in the congregational case studies in the next chapter.

In the meantime, we did some more work with the data. The examination of the range of scores for individual responders in churches ranked by Missional Quotient reveals a significant gap in the perception of congregational members regarding the prevalence of behaviors breeding mistrust in their local congregations. While the overall congregational trust scores are all above 60, indicating a culture of "Trust" or "Strong Trust," some individual responders' scores were down in the "Mistrust" range and even into the "Strong Mistrust" range. In other words, there are quite a few dissenters from the majority opinion in these churches.

The behavior most contributing to mistrust in the UBIC congregations surveyed was forming cliques. Other behaviors scoring low on the scale were gossip, making decisions affecting others without involving others, and looking out for one's own interests. The behavior observed the least in the UBIC congregations surveyed was openly attacking others. Other behaviors that were rarely observed were trying to get even with others, intimidating others, and trying to discredit others.

WHAT WE FOUND: PASTORS FEEL THE RESISTANCE

Since resistance to change occurs on many different levels besides the relational resistance tested in the Congregational Trust Survey, the pastors' follow-up questionnaire contained 30 statements pertaining to various dimensions of resistance. It should be noted that this calculation merely reflects the perception and observations of the pastors of the churches of the prevalence of resistance in his or her congregation. Dimensions of resistance with a percentage equal to 50% or greater were classified as "strong resistance" and a percentage between 1 and 49 was classified as "some resistance."

The responses from the pastors' survey were very enlightening in revealing the perceived depth of resistance to change in some UBIC congregations. The questions dealt with missional change initiatives in the congregations surveyed, the perception of the pastor regarding the resistance or readiness of the congregation for change, the types of resistance encountered, and the reactions on the part of congregants to the Trust Survey itself. As was expected, pastors reported more incidents of resistance in congregations with lower trust scores.

The dimensions of resistance that were shown to have the highest percentage of incidents from the responses to the pastors' follow-up questionnaires were emotional and behavioral resistance. Pastors reported that a satisfaction with the status quo and emotional withdrawal were the predominant forms of emotional resistance. Behavioral resistance took the form of people leaving the church, members withholding financial contributions, and people verbally attacking each other. The most prevalent form of behavioral resistance was reported to be "feet dragging" in U.S. UBIC churches.

Pastors also reported incidents of relational and mental resistance in the UBIC churches. Most of the mental resistance consisted of not having enough information to understand the rationale for a change and not knowing if a change would really work in their church. The relational resistance was evidenced by complaints that pastors were always trying to ram change down their throats and that church leaders were not really listening to what they were saying or comprehending what they were feeling.

Spiritual resistance did not appear to be an issue in most churches. People were not using the Bible to substantiate their views concerning change, nor were they calling for a return to biblical patterns for congregational life and work. Only two churches reported spiritual warfare going on in the midst of the resistance.

WHAT WE FOUND: A SUMMARY

In this study we found some things that surprised us. First, all of the churches surveyed, regardless of size, rated themselves to be above the median in terms of trust levels in the congregation. Without a larger sample to compare against, we're not sure if this means that our sample is biased because only trusting churches would allow such questions to be asked among them, or if this merely indicates that a modicum of trust is necessary to continuing functioning as a congregation. We decided that we could still compare trust levels in a meaningful way and continued our research.

Second, there is no clear correlation between how the churches described their level of internal trust and what their patterns of growth reveal about their missional orientation. This was most surprising, given all that we've read and experienced on this topic. But these results do not necessarily mean that no such correlation exists; it is possible that the initiation of efforts to move from maintenance to missional may, in itself, lower trust scores in some churches and, conversely, the lack of such efforts may result in a high level of trust but a poor missional orientation.

In order to better understand the relationship between mission and trust, we need to look past the numbers and get some sense of what is happening on the ground. The pastors' survey helped us do that. In fact, it confirmed our assumption that there is more resistance when a leader is initiating missional change, and it explained a bit of what kinds of resistance are more likely to show up.

In addition to the pastors' survey, we completed a number of congregational case studies, a few of which are shared in the next chapter. These give us a more vivid picture of how trust and mission interact in the life of a local church.

PART THREE

Re-Energizing

7

Maintenance or Mission

One of These Churches May Be Yours

WHY CASE STUDIES?

PEOPLE WHO DO SERIOUS scholarly research distinguish between quantitative research (the kind that involves numbers) and qualitative research (the kind that involves the gathering of stories, impressions, and other observations). Both of these are considered "primary research," which is done first-hand by the researcher him or herself, as opposed to "secondary research," which is studying the work of others. In this volume, we have offered all kinds. Chapters 3 and 4 constitute the bulk of the secondary research, although other learning from sources is scattered throughout the book. In chapter 6, we presented the results of our extensive quantitative research. But data can take us only so far. And so we have dug more deeply and offered some case studies of individual congregations or personal experiences that amplify or clarify what we have learned from other methods. These include our own stories, which are found in chapters 2 and 5, the vignettes which opened our discussion in chapter 1, and now the case studies in this chapter.

These stories emerged from the data received from our congregational survey. The information we offer here is derived from 1) the responses of members of the congregation to the Congregational Trust Survey, 2) the responses of the pastors of these congregations to the survey instrument distributed to them, 3) the data collected from a decadal study of each congregation's annual reports, and 4) follow-up conversations with church leaders, when necessary, to clarify patterns and behaviors. These stories collectively illustrate the complexity of congregational life and the multiple factors that influence both trust and receptivity to mission. They also point to certain commonalities that will be examined a bit more fully in chapter 8.

Note that each church is identified by a pseudonym. Our intent here is not to dwell on the particulars of any given situation but to note patterns that you may, in some cases, find familiar. We did. We have intentionally identified congregations that fit each of the patterns of correlation between trust and mission that we identified in the data results.

COUNTRYSIDE CHURCH

An attempt at implementing a second service to provide a place in the church for people wanting a contemporary style of worship resulted in the loss of people on both sides of the issue from Countryside Church. Almost 20 percent of the congregation strongly opposed contemporary worship music and a second service, while nearly 20 percent of the congregation strongly favored the plan. After nearly a year of discussions, the pastor thought that the congregation was ready to launch the second service, but strong opposition began involving many false accusations, withdrawal of financial support, divisiveness, and negativity, and people on both sides became very angry and left the church. As a result, the people who remained were very fearful of and resistant to change.

This congregation is located in a rural area of a southern state. The congregants prided themselves in being a small, rural church that was not at all like big city churches. People (including the pastor) who moved into the area were referred to as "Outsiders" and the pastor had been referred to on numerous occasions as a "D___ Yankee" and as a "Skinhead." The pastor reported that, from his observation of other churches in that area, it generally took between five to ten years for people to begin to trust outsiders.

Countryside Church increased 30 percent in worship attendance during the last five years of the 1990s, but through the decade of the 2000s, the congregation dropped nearly 50 percent. They recorded 68 conversions and 58 baptisms in a 15 year period. During eight of those years, the number of reported conversions was higher than the national average for churches comparable in size, and during five of those years, the number of baptisms exceeded the national average. The survey results indicated the lowest level of trust, with forming cliques, springing surprises, and using information for one's advantage being observed the most. There is a clear link in this case of an atmosphere of mistrust leading to resistance to change.

NEW LIFE CHURCH

New Life Church has been serving a rural community outside of a small Pennsylvania city for over eighty years. Many faithful pastors have served this flock, with many conversions and baptisms through the years. Over the past decade, however, it has shifted into a survival mindset, with a shrinking congregation and dwindling finances, and significant pull back from earlier efforts to engage its community. There are hopeful signs, however, that growth and greater outreach will return.

In the latter years of the 1990s, the church was growing steadily with strong conversion growth, membership commitments, and baptisms. A Community Care Center was established, offering counseling, health screenings, computer training, and other services to the community, and a wing was built onto the church facility to accommodate these outreach ministries. The senior pastor and youth pastor were bi-vocational, and an associate pastor was added to the staff to provide ministry leadership and congregational care.

The senior pastor left in 2000 to lead a church planting effort in a neighboring community, specifically targeting people who were disenchanted with traditional churches, and the associate pastor was promoted into the senior pastor's role. His tenure was short, as the church dropped in size to less than half of what it was in the previous ten years and the Community Care Center activities were cut back. The youth pastor became the interim senior pastor, and under his eighteen-month leadership, the church grew eight percent with conversions, baptisms, and new members.

I (Paul) became the interim preaching pastor in 2003 and served until early 2007. I was most impressed that all of the local church ministries were led by members of the congregation. The Pastoral Relations Commission made it clear during my interview that all that was needed from a pastor was to preach during the Sunday morning worship service and other special events during the year and to provide emergency pastoral care to members who were hospitalized. Since I lived over 45 minutes away from the church and worked a full-time job, it was not feasible for me to do much more than preaching and minimal visitation. One of the members took care of the regular visitation of homebound members. A part-time music director led blended worship services and directed a choir for special events. Members of the congregation were involved regularly in community-wide events, which gave the church positive exposure to the local residents. Small groups were held each week, led by members of the church, and the Community Care Center was being utilized by various local organizations. During my ministry, the church averaged annual growth of four percent with minimal conversions and baptisms.

When we evaluated the results of the survey for this congregation, they actually scored fairly high in trust. The behaviors that were most frequently observed were withholding information, giving more negative feedback than positive, using manipulative tactics, looking out for one's own interests, seeking "win-lose" outcomes, and pretending to agree with others. The behaviors that were rarely observed were openly attacking each other and putting each other down.

One positive development occurred during my ministry at New Life Church. Another small struggling United Brethren church three miles down the road needed a pastor, and we were able to enter into a cooperative agreement with that congregation to "share" my preaching ministry on Sunday mornings. It was a win-win situation for me and for the churches, as both congregations were struggling financially.

There were a number of forms of resistance evident during my tenure as interim pastor. Some resistance surfaced when an attempt was made to hire youth directors as a community outreach ministry. Most of the unwillingness stemmed from uncertainty over why someone would be hired when volunteers had been leading the efforts all along. While lay people led all of the ministries, there seemed to be a sense of everything being on autopilot, with everyone faithfully doing their jobs. However, not a whole lot of reflection was going on over why they were doing what they were doing and how fruitful those efforts had been in accomplishing the mission of the church.

When I presented in a board meeting the results of the Trust Survey and information about church decadal growth trends, I encouraged the members to reflect on current church practices and the fruitfulness of their efforts. I was attempting to move the discussion toward changes that would need to be made to communicate the Gospel more effectively to an unchurched population. One member became very defensive, questioning if all of the hard work that had been done had been in vain. There was an overall sense that if the church members were faithful in doing what they had always been doing, God would reward those efforts. There was little desire to change what, in their minds, was working quite well, in spite of the evidence that little true conversion growth was being accomplished.

In the years following my ministry there, two part-time pastors have served the congregation. Sunday morning attendance has declined 29 percent with 2 conversions and 1 baptism reported. In the summer of 2012, a female pastor was hired who is strengthening the small group discipleship ministries and is leading the congregation in reaching out to the community. With much prayer, we trust the Lord for new life in this once vibrant church.

GOOD SHEPHERD CHURCH

Good Shepherd Church is located in a county seat in a Midwestern state. The church began in a tent revival in 1949 and has grown to a congregation of around 100 people.

They held a six-week "Kids in the Park" program to reach out to unchurched children in place of their regular Wednesday night program. The children who normally attended the church program formed the core group for this outreach ministry, and they were successful in sharing the Gospel with 10 children who did not normally attend church. The program "petered out" during the fifth and sixth weeks, so they did not have the turnout they hoped for on the last night, which was a picnic for the children and parents. To the best of the pastor's knowledge, the outreach program did not succeed in moving any of these unchurched families into his congregation, but it was successful in the sense that 10 children heard the Gospel message and accepted Christ as Savior.

Initial resistance to the outreach program manifested itself mostly in feet dragging and "we tried that before and it did not work." The pastor was also accused of making a unilateral decision to implement this program before consulting the Christian Education chairperson. This individual was not averse to the idea of this program but felt that she should have been consulted prior to any decision being made. From the pastor's comments on the survey, it appeared that the resistance to change was rooted in a few power-holders in the church who were undermining his leadership effectiveness by the comments they were making to other members in the church.

Good Shepherd Church has experienced a 40 percent increase in attendance over a 15 year period, with 254 conversions and 146 baptisms. The results from the Trust Survey were in the mid-level of strong trust, despite reports of gossiping, making decisions affecting others without involving others, and springing surprises on others. This case confirms our assumption that missional churches have higher levels of trust. While resistance to change was not widespread in this congregation, there appeared to be pockets of resistance that bore watching.

GREEN PASTURES CHURCH

Evangelism classes with actual fieldwork were started in Green Pastures Church to give members experience in sharing the Gospel and distributing tracts. The pastor reported that the emphasis on fellowship and worship in the church had eclipsed outreach and the classes were a means of encouraging more of an outward focus. The pastor modeled an outward focus for his congregation by joining a blues band in the community and starting a guitar repair business. He stated that these community activities helped to get him out of the "pastoral bubble" of ministering only to church people. The congregation had not been totally on board with the emphasis on evangelism and had resisted any efforts that disrupted comfortable routines or that required too much of a time commitment.

Green Pastures Church was located in a rural area of Central Pennsylvania and experienced an overall decline in attendance and membership in its last ten years of existence. However, during those years, thirteen conversions and twenty-five baptisms were recorded. Their conversion growth never exceeded the national average for small churches, but for one year, the number of baptisms exceeded the national average.

When the Congregational Trust Survey was administered to the church, the overall score indicated the highest level of strong trust. Behaviors that were most contributing to mistrust were looking out for one's own interests, springing surprises on others, and gossiping. Behaviors that were never observed in this congregation were trying to get even with others and openly attacking one another. Behaviors that were observed very rarely were trying to discredit others, putting each other down, and trying to intimidate others. With such high levels of trust, one would think the church would have been ripe for growth, but instead Green Pastures closed its doors and merged with another congregation.

CONTENTMENT CHAPEL

Contentment Chapel is a small church located in a major metropolitan area that has evidenced little growth over the past 15 years. At the beginning of the study period, the church had an average of 27 in attendance and fifteen years later had 23 attending, which represents an overall decline of 15 percent. The church did report 17 conversions and seven baptisms during those 15 years.

The church had attempted to implement missional change in the early 2000s. The pastor reported that he had attempted to launch, with the assistance of a retired state police officer, a ministry to young people in the community since no young people were attending the church at that time. The administrative board had approved the launch of the program and allowed the use of the fellowship building but there was no other assistance offered by any of the members of the church or board. The pastor indicated that the congregation was neutral toward the proposed change, with little initial resistance to the idea but little willingness to get behind the proposal either. However, he reported that there had been some resistance in the forms of emotional withdrawal, feet-dragging, and blank stares. Some objected to the plan for financial reasons, believing that they did not possess the resources to support the ministry. The pastor was also offered conflicting feedback, with some saying that such a plan had been tried before but it did not work, while others said that they had never tried an idea like that before.

The pastor's overall assessment of his congregational members was that they were highly resistant to change. He had served the congregation for 13 years and most of the members liked the church the way it was. They did not want to change their comfortable routines and traditions, objected to pastors wanting to "ram change down their throats," and insisted that they would never change. They were also afflicted with exclusivist attitudes toward newcomers. The pastor reported that over the years of his ministry, many new people had attended but they had not stayed long, not having been made to feel welcomed or included. He described the church as "one big family clique."

The congregation had the lowest congregational score on the Trust Survey recorded for this research. The behaviors observed which contribute to mistrust were forming cliques, criticizing others, looking out for one's own interests, gossip, making excuses for mistakes, and inconsistent messaging. This church confirms that a lack of trust would be prevalent in churches showing little growth.

FELLOWSHIP CHAPEL

Fellowship Chapel is located in a suburb of the capital of a Midwestern state. The church was started as a church plant in 1960, met for a time in the home of two of its members, and then moved to their current site in 1964. Over the past 15 years, they have averaged 64 in worship attendance.

The pastor reported that his congregation had implemented small group fellowships with short-term commitments. The small groups met in people's homes once a week for six weeks and they experienced positive "inreach and outreach" through this new ministry. The pastor noted that the people were somewhat willing in the implementation of this change and the only reported resistance was in feet-dragging, blank stares, the reaction that "we've never done that before," and questions about the benefits of the change for individuals and families.

The pastor was proactive before implementing this change by bringing in leaders from another church the people respected, who talked with the congregation about the benefits of small groups. This reduced the potential resistance to the missional change initiative and built greater trust within the congregation. Currently they have small groups for people with disabilities and for inmates in the county prison. Other groups gather around common interests such as tennis, music, and baking. They also have small groups for sportsmen and senior citizens.

Fellowship Chapel's worship attendance declined 18 percent in 15 years with 134 conversions and 30 baptisms reported. The results of the Trust Survey showed a reasonable level of trust within the congregation. Behaviors contributing most to mistrust were gossiping, making excuses, blaming others for mistakes, and springing surprises on each other. Behaviors rarely observed in this congregation were openly attacking and undercutting others, and trying to discredit others. What surprised us most in our analysis of this congregation was that while the level of trust was good, there was not a greater readiness to accept the initiative to implement the small groups. We are gratified, however, to see the positive acceptance of this initiative over the past five years, with so many conversions and baptisms. The kingdom of God is growing in the Midwest.

SHADOW VALLEY CHURCH

Shadow Valley Church is over 80 years old, located in a rural area. When an interim bi-vocational pastor accepted the call to that church following years of decline, the board members made it clear that they liked the old-time hymns and traditional worship services. They thought that the niche they could best fill would be to provide a traditional service for those who were disenchanted with attempts at implementing contemporary music in other churches. Their previous pastor had served faithfully for many years despite a steady decline in attendance, and the congregation was averaging 20 in Sunday morning worship when he resigned. The new interim pastor felt strongly that the key to renewal in the church would be in developing a Sunday morning service that would be strong in teaching and in music. He brought in a part-time director of music and together they crafted a traditional service that attracted unchurched families, and the church began to grow. Over time, they gradually introduced elements of a contemporary nature into the worship service, but these were accepted because trust was building as the members saw how the church was growing.

Shadow Valley Church had declined in attendance by 92 percent in the decade studied, but had recorded 49 conversions and 19 baptisms during that same time frame. However, there was a 39 percent rise in attendance in the year the survey was administered. It was experiencing a turnaround and was showing signs of becoming a strong missional congregation with great potential for further growth. Though the church had strong initial resistance to change, the pastor and church leaders built up a good deal of "trust capital" through the successful implementation of missional change.

Many new ministries were initiated and implemented by members of the congregation, which resulted in people seeking the Lord, such as a ministry to teenagers (at a time when no teenagers were attending the church), a pen pal ministry to prisoners, and a women's fellowship. One school-teacher had a special burden for children (at a time when no children were attending the church) and began a pre-school ministry using the church facility that reached out to over 30 young families in the community. An impressive playground was constructed on the church property, which was a visible indication to the community that the church cared about children. A number of families with no prior church involvement began attending the worship services and eventually joined the membership. Special activities sponsored by the pre-school, such as the annual "Hallelujah Hoedown" and the Christmas pageant touched hundreds of people in the community

Leading Missional Change

and gave many of them their first positive exposure to Christians who truly loved God and each other.

When the Trust Survey was administered to the congregation during that season of turn around, they ranked in the highest level of strong trust. Some of the behaviors fostering mistrust observed most frequently were making decisions affecting others without involving others, gossiping about others, looking out for one's own interests, and focusing on other's mistakes. No one had ever observed any intimidation in the congregation and behaviors rarely observed were seeking win-lose outcomes and blaming others for mistakes.

When a new bi-vocational pastor was called two years later, momentum was building and the future looked bright for this congregation. The new pastor had strong gifts of teaching, mercy, and evangelism, and many new families were joining, mostly through the ministry of the pre-school. However, a spiritual battle was raging beneath the surface. During the time of pastoral transition, one new influential family had been attempting to introduce charismatic-style worship elements into the morning service, and also became entrenched in the administration of the pre-school. When the new pastor sought to bring the pre-school back under the direct oversight of the church board two years later, passive aggression erupted into all-out warfare. Gossip, public attacks, political maneuvering, criticism, and intimidation were the order of the day, but in the end, those who were at the root of the problem were removed from the membership. However, many others left the church at the same time, and the pastor and board were left with the task of rebuilding the church and trust. Our prayer for the Shadow Valley Church is that the congregation will recover its sense of mission, and that the current pastor will not grow weary.

FRESH BREEZE CHURCH

The winds of revival are blowing in Fresh Breeze Church, a mid-western congregation in a small rural town of 200 residents. For 15 years, they had an average worship attendance of 26, but in recent years, they more than doubled to an average attendance of 55.

When the Trust Survey was administered, this congregation recorded one of the highest scores of the participating churches. This high level of trust was surprising in that it came on the heels of a decade of decline. The congregation had experienced a 43 percent drop in Sunday worship attendance, but recorded 14 conversions and 12 baptisms during that same time frame. Some of the behaviors fostering mistrust observed most frequently were giving more negative feedback than positive, looking out for one's own interests, and pretending to agree with others. One of the responders seemed desirous of protecting the reputation of the church and entered a note at the bottom of the survey, "I trust my church family with my heart and soul and life. I love them all and would do anything for them."

The pastor at the time of the survey affirmed that members of the church truly did trust each other implicitly. He had served the church for two years and had been impressed with the depths of relationships among members of the church. Trust was not a problem within the church family itself, but a lack of trust was an issue in the community toward the church and its former pastors. The pastor indicated that the main factor contributing to a lack of growth in the church was the perception of the church in the surrounding area. The church is located in a small, very rural town with residents who all know each other and know each other's business. In the late 1990s, a former pastor of the church attempted to contact inactive members to encourage them to either attend church or take their names off of the roll. This created a good deal of animosity in the community toward the pastor. Another former pastor was embroiled in a lawsuit with a member of the church.

The good news is that a turnaround is occurring in this congregation. Not only are they experiencing an increase in worship attendance, conversions, and baptisms, but their website shows evidence of a desire to partner with community groups with plans to restore the local park.

YOUR STORY HERE

If we were to write the story of your congregation here, what would we have to tell? Perhaps you'd like to give that a try yourself. Take the empty space below and write a first draft, noting patterns of growth or decline in the past 10–15 years, major accomplishments and disappointments, your own observations about how trust is or is not expressed in your congregation, and your sense of where the church is at this point in time. What prayers do you have for this congregation as you look forward? What does God want to do?

8

Your Mission, If You Choose to Accept It

Living Like a Follower of Jesus

WHAT WE WERE TRYING TO DO

THIS PROJECT EXAMINED A significant problem facing many American pastors and church leaders—congregational resistance to missional change. Leaders who desire the advancement of the Kingdom of God may be frustrated by resistance to change because they see the needs of people in their communities who do not yet know Christ, and they constantly explore new ways of sharing the Gospel with them. However, in many cases, congregational members resist change because they like their church just the way it is. Many resist any efforts to change even if it means that new opportunities to evangelize the lost and to disciple new converts may be missed. That's what we've experienced in our own ministries at times, and that's what we hear from many of our friends and colleagues.

Our purpose was to explore the roots of congregational resistance to missional change and to search for ways to change a congregation's dominant culture from resistance to change to readiness for change. The primary hypothesis, based upon a study of literature from the business community, was that the key issue in overcoming resistance to change might be relational. Therefore, we sought to determine whether or not congregants are

Your Mission, If You Choose to Accept It

more likely to embrace missional change if there is a strong environment of trust within the congregation.

During this project, congregations were surveyed to determine levels of trust to see if any connection existed between that trust and congregational readiness to change. We assumed that churches with higher levels of trust would have greater readiness to change. We also assumed that "change" in such situations would be in the direction of a fuller mission orientation and, therefore, that such change would experience greater growth and higher conversion rates. We further assumed that churches with lower levels of trust would have greater resistance to change and, therefore, more difficulty with growth and lower conversion rates. Closely tied to the connection between trust and readiness to change was the question of how levels of trust and levels of resistance to change were related to the missional orientation of a congregation. As we have noted, not all of these assumptions were correct, but we did learn some valuable lessons about the process of initiating and implementing missional change, and in this chapter we discuss those implications, so you and your congregation can benefit from this research.

WHAT WE FOUND

The results from the Congregational Trust Survey (Appendix A) and the pastors' follow-up questionnaire (Appendix B) confirmed a correlation between high trust scores and less resistance to change. Churches with lower trust scores showed evidence of greater prevalence of different forms of resistance than churches with higher trust scores.

The pastors' follow-up questionnaire responses revealed that instances of emotional and behavioral resistance were more prevalent in the studied churches than instances of mental or relational resistance. Only two churches reported spiritual warfare going on in the midst of implementing missional change. This low number of churches reporting spiritual warfare was a surprise to the researchers. When congregations are moving ahead with changes to better fulfill the purposes of God and to advance the work of the Kingdom of God, there is often a sense of spiritual opposition. In terms of relational dynamics in times of conflict, this is important. Pastors and other church leaders should remember that their "struggle is not against flesh and blood, but against the rulers, against the authorities, against the powers of this dark world, and against the spiritual forces of evil in the heavenly realms" (Eph. 6:12).

Further research is needed to determine whether or not higher trust scores necessarily indicate greater readiness for change. One of the assumptions of this project was that less resistance to change would mean greater readiness to change, but that may not always be the case. Churches seeking to implement missional change could find that the dynamics of the change effort would increase mistrust leading to more resistance than readiness. The congregational case studies in chapter 7 showed churches with high scores on the trust scale, indicating only that behaviors that build mistrust were not widely observed in that church. There were, however, high levels of resistance to missional change attempts in those churches. The Congregational Trust Survey we used was limited in that it only asked questions about the behaviors that breed mistrust. A modified trust survey that would query congregants concerning the behaviors that build trust may be a more helpful tool in answering the question of the linkage between high trust and readiness for change.

One thing that has been clearly shown, both in the review of the literature and in the results of the Congregational Trust Survey, is that readiness to change cannot be fostered by the mere absence of behaviors that breed mistrust. A number of congregations with high scores on the Congregational Trust Survey showed high levels of resistance to change. To foster readiness for change within a congregation, pastors and church leaders need to concentrate consistent, extended effort on behaviors that foster trust, especially in the areas where mistrust has been shown to be an issue in the churches. Trust is not built instantaneously, and the more mistrust is ingrained within a congregation, the longer it takes to rebuild trust.

One of the questions we sought to answer was whether or not churches with a high missional orientation would have the highest scores on the Congregational Trust Survey. When the trust scores of congregations were compared with churches with a comparable missional orientation, the congregations on a maintenance level actually scored a bit higher than missional churches. The five "Strong Missional" churches did have the highest congregational trust scores with an average score of 105, but when the individual scores in these churches were averaged, the mean score was 98. The eleven "Missional" churches had the lowest congregational average score of 96, but when the individual scores in these churches were averaged, the mean score was 89. The six "Strong Maintenance" churches had congregational and individual averages of 101 and the seven "Maintenance" churches had a congregational average of 103 and individual averages of 102. When all of the "Maintenance" and "Strong Maintenance" individual scores were averaged together, the mean score was 102, while the combination of the trust scores of "Missional" and "Strong Missional" was only 92. This was a major surprise as it was assumed that the congregations with the highest missional orientation would score the highest in trust and would, therefore, have greater readiness for missional change.

We have pondered this at some length and depth, and noticed some interesting and helpful patterns. For instance, some churches that did not attempt to implement any kind of missional changes had high levels of trust. An example is "Church 4555" (all churches in the survey were coded like this), which was classified as a "Maintenance" church. The pastor reported that no changes had been attempted in the congregation in the prior year. Nevertheless, the church scored 109 on the Trust Scale, which was in the 91st percentile. It would be interesting to rerun the Trust Survey in this congregation after attempts are made to implement change to determine if trust levels would be negatively impacted by disruptions to the status quo.

We also noted that churches that are attempting to move into a more missional orientation are more likely to experience greater resistance to change and lower levels of trust. The literature we reviewed indicated that trust could be built through the successful implementation of change[1] but also warned that some organizations attempting to implement transformational changes may experience a diminishment in the levels of trust.[2] The diminishment of trust due to change was confirmed in the experience of Church 7981. The pastor had attempted the implementation of a contemporary worship service in addition to the traditional worship service. The growth rates of the church indicated a need for a second service and a strong nucleus of younger families gave the impetus for providing a worship experience that would better reach a younger generation. The resistance that arose over this missional change was manifested in numerous behaviors that eroded trust in the church leadership. As noted in chapter 5, I (Tony) had a very similar experience early in my ministry career.

It is possible that the churches that are willing to take the greatest risks in reaching the lost are those whose members put their trust in each other to the test and risk exposure to more incidents of resistance. One of the

---

1. Lines et al, "The production of trust."
2. Maurer, *Why Resistance Matters*; O'Toole, *Leading Change*.

participating pastors from a missional church said that "if the group trusts the pastor/staff and feels they have researched/prayed, the amount of resistance is minimal. As long as they believe [the pastor and staff] have their best interests at heart, they don't feel that every detail has to be what they would have chosen." This attitude is reflective of a more spiritually mature congregation than many of our colleagues serve.

Another possible explanation for lower trust scores in churches with higher missional orientation could be the speed at which the congregation attempts to implement missional change. When church leaders move too quickly at implementing change without adequate preparation, members may respond with resistance, while those who prepare the congregation for the change may find greater readiness because of higher trust.[3]

An example of resistance due to leaders attempting to implement change too quickly was shown in the case study of Church 3676. The pastor attempted to move the congregation prematurely into a building program. The church facility had limited seating and parking and was situated on a very dangerous intersection. Several children had narrow escapes with vehicles entering church property to by-pass the intersection, which necessitated the blocking off of one of the entrances to the parking lot. A feasibility study by a consultant hired by the congregation indicated that the time was right to move forward with a capital campaign. However, some underlying trust issues revealed by the feasibility study had been left unaddressed by the church leadership. Therefore, conflict in the congregation ultimately led to the retirement of the senior pastor.

An example of readiness for change due to the proactive preparation of a congregation for that change may be found in the experience of Church 9601. The church leaders implemented a short-term small group ministry, which resulted in "positive inreach and outreach." The pastor prepared the congregation for this change by bringing in leaders whom the congregation respected from other churches. These leaders shared with the congregation the positive benefits their churches received through the implementation of small groups. The proactive approach of the pastors and leaders helped to prepare the church for the change and built trust in the leaders.

By way of contrast, the experience of Church 7981 illustrates that proactive preparation for missional change does not always result in readiness. The pastor reported that congregational discussions were held for over a year prior to the implementation of a contemporary worship service but

---

3. Kouzes and Posner, *Leadership Challenge*.

that strong resistance did not manifest itself until the leaders were ready to implement the new service. It is possible that time taken to prepare some congregations for change may provide the leaders of the resistance with an opportunity to entrench their positions and load their weapons.

Many congregational members realize that pastors and church leaders really do have the best interests of the congregation at heart. Many are convinced that their leaders are committed to moving the church forward and advancing the mission of the Kingdom of God. The climate of trust arising from the practice of behaviors that foster trust may build a strong readiness for missional change.

HOW DO WE KNOW IF WE'RE MISSIONAL?

The question of whether or not it was possible to accurately assess the missional orientation of a congregation through the analysis of attendance and other statistics was raised as a result of this project. A review of the comments of pastors in the follow-up questionnaires indicated that statistical analysis alone was insufficient for determining missional orientation. One of the key lessons learned has been the realization that each church is a unique organism and that all attempts at classification according to size or orientation are mere guesses at best. The perspectives of those who are serving "in the trenches" may offset the statistical factors that appear to indicate a missional orientation in some congregations. By the same token, the perspectives of those serving "in the trenches" may be too subjective to offer a clear picture of the ministry realities in that context. In addition, the potential misclassification of congregations according to missional orientation may have impacted the conclusions drawn from the statistical analysis of the Trust Survey results. Statistical analysis is helpful in seeing trends over a period of time in a congregation, but change occurs so rapidly in this world and a congregation's readiness to adapt to change may vary considerably, depending upon current circumstances.

The question then arises concerning the possibility that there could be other research tools that might more accurately assess the missional orientation of a congregation. The awareness of the changing needs in the surrounding culture and the proactivity of the congregation to address those changing needs may not be able to be objectively measured. However, a congregational survey of the depth of its community awareness and an inquiry concerning the perception of the pastor and other church leaders of the speed of congregational adaptation to community needs may be better predictors of missional orientation. A community survey of the perspective of outsiders regarding the reputation and community involvement of a congregation could provide an even more objective analysis of the missional orientation of that local church.

The assessment of missional orientation could be complicated by the degree of resistance or readiness to recent changes in a congregation. Kenneth Hultman, who provided the Trust Survey used in our study, has also created a "Change Opinion Survey,"[4] which could be a valuable instrument for objectively measuring various dimensions of readiness and resistance within a congregation that is considering a missional change or that has recently implemented a change. A history of successful implementations of missional changes or the evidence of the congregational benefits from those changes would also be helpful in assessing missional orientation.

Another strategy to determine missional orientation might be evaluating the alignment of values and norms within a congregation. Again, Hultman may have something to offer us. His "Megavalue Scale"[5] could be a valuable instrument for a congregation to see the true values of its members regarding integrity, honesty, genuineness, concern for others, and acceptance of others. A comparison of the results of the "Megavalue Scale" with the espoused beliefs and practices of a congregation would give a better picture of the direction the congregation is headed.

Another indicator of missional orientation comes from the denominational attendance and membership records. The number of members on the church roll is higher than the number of regular attendees in the weekly worship services in 65% of the maintenance churches but in only 35% of the missional churches. The missional churches averaged 11% fewer members on their roll than weekly attendees at worship, while the maintenance churches averaged 10% more members than weekly attendees. This was an interesting discovery, as maintaining members on a church roll, despite their lack of involvement in the life of the church, reinforces the impression that maintenance churches are in a survival mode. The pastor of Church 4300 attempted to remove inactive members from the church roll and subsequently experienced the wrath of the former members and residents of the community. Lay leaders of maintenance churches may not want to alienate people they hope to win back to the church by removing them

4. Hultman, *Making change irresistible*.
5. Ibid.

Your Mission, If You Choose to Accept It

from a membership roster, so they allow those names to remain indefinitely on the roll. This phenomenon also hints that the maintenance churches may often be rural "community" or "family" congregations, in which inactive members are related to active members.

The emphasis of missional churches regarding membership, however, is on the personal involvement of every member in mission. An "inactive member" is an oxymoron in a truly missional church. Churches that grow primarily by attracting people to worship events may not be missional at all, if those worshippers are not discipled and serving. A "seeker" model of ministry may be effective in introducing nonbelievers to the love of God, but can result in a failure to move those individuals beyond spectator status in the Church or beyond spiritual infancy in their walk with God. A missional approach to ministry, whatever the size of the congregation, is rooted in engaging the entire body of Christ, to the degree possible, in God's mission in the world.

An important corollary lesson learned through this project is the danger of equating missional orientation with attendance growth in local congregations. It is not difficult to attain a 5% increase each year in attendance, especially if the new attendees are transfers from another congregation. Transfer growth is not necessarily Kingdom growth and definitely not an evidence of a missional orientation. In fact, churches with a missional mindset may become smaller as they seek to build the Kingdom. When a church "gives away" families for the start of a church plant or to help struggling congregations, they are fulfilling the missional mandate of the Church. When key leaders in a congregation sense the call of God upon their lives to serve on a foreign field or to shepherd a flock in God's fields and the church sends them out with a blessing, the church is showing evidence of a missional orientation. Likewise, when a missional pastor leads a congregation into a new vision for the congregation, some people may leave, but this does not necessarily mean that the vision is wrong. Jesus had the same problem.

Congregational involvement in outreach ministries may not produce dazzling conversion statistics but those efforts do help to build the Kingdom. Seeking opportunities to have spiritual conversations with seekers, loving the lost, discipling new converts in the faith, and equipping them for mission are tasks that are time-consuming and labor-intensive. When these new converts are not assimilated into the local congregation and church growth is not evident, many long-term members may grumble that outreach ministries are not generating new members for the church and may demand that their leaders and members use their time and financial resources more wisely. However, in spite of the lack of growth in the congregation, the Kingdom is being advanced and that is what is most important in view of eternity.

BEHAVIORS THAT DAMAGE TRUST

One thing that has been clearly shown, both in the review of the literature and in the results of the Congregational Trust Survey, is that readiness to change cannot be fostered by the mere absence of behaviors that breed mistrust. A number of congregations with high scores on the Congregational Trust Survey showed high levels of resistance to change. To foster readiness for change within a congregation, pastors and church leaders need to concentrate their efforts on behaviors that foster trust[6] and be willing to do so consistently over a long period of time. Trust is not built instantaneously, and the more mistrust is ingrained within a congregation, the longer it takes to rebuild trust. In chapter 4 we discussed a number of the factors that breed mistrust. Let us now turn our attention to the more positive side of that question: How can missional leaders build trust? Following are ten suggestions emerging from this research.

First, do what you say you will do. A significant problem unearthed through the Congregational Trust Survey was people making agreements they do not keep. The Scriptures warn against making promises to God that are not kept (Eccles. 5:5–6) and command people to be sure to do whatever they say they will do (Deut. 23:23). The example of Annanias and Sapphira (Acts 5) offers a powerful warning of the disastrous consequences of attempting to deceive God and fellow-members of the church. When God's people keep their word to others, they are following the example of Christ who had "no deceit in his mouth" (1 Pet. 2:22; Rev. 14:5). Therefore, pastors desiring to build trust must be careful about the way they communicate with church members. Keeping promises, being consistent in the messages they give to people, and refraining from slander and gossip are critical to building trust. Using words to build up rather than to tear down fosters trust. Affirming the contributions and accomplishments of others

---

6. For a listing of the behaviors that build trust, please visit the companion website to this book at www.leadingmissionalchange.info

and praising Christ-honoring character often encourages similar behavior in others, fostering an atmosphere of trust.

Second, acknowledge mistakes. Behaviors relating to the handling of the mistakes of others also scored low on the trust scale. The two that had lower scores were blaming others for mistakes and focusing on the mistakes of others. The way that pastors handle their own mistakes, as well as the mistakes of others, can have a powerful impact on the trust of the congregation in them. When people see pastors admitting to their own mistakes and taking responsibility for the outcomes of decisions they make instead of blaming others, people are less likely to be suspicious of them. Congregations must be cautious in how they deal with people who have made mistakes. Gentleness and forgiveness should mark these encounters. Calls for reconciliation and repentance are vital in reestablishing relationships with God and with others, but these calls must be made in meekness and humility. Recognizing one's own proclivity to err can go a long way in building trust among members.

Third, address problems. Congregational leaders and pastors must not allow destructive behaviors to continue. When the behaviors that breed mistrust are permitted and people are not held accountable for their actions, trust is eroded within the congregation. When leaders are not willing to allow negative behaviors to go unaddressed within the congregation but hold people accountable for their decisions and behaviors, a climate of solid trust is built. The implementation of church discipline, according to the model of Matthew 15:15–18, is a good starting point for pastors and church leaders. When a simple verbal correction, done privately, does not succeed in changing behavior, then the next step of taking several witnesses to confront the wrong behavior needs to be taken. The entire point of church discipline is to restore the repentant so that when repentance is evident, the church leadership is ready to affirm their forgiveness and restore to fellowship those who have repented.

Fourth, affirm often. Instead of focusing on the negative behaviors that breed mistrust, pastors and church leaders should praise and affirm those congregational members who are practicing the behaviors that foster trust. People act according to what is rewarded and encouraged. Actions that are rewarded get repeated.[7] It is essential that pastors and leaders affirm those who are engaged in mission within their local congregations and communities. Public recognition of people engaged in various avenues of

---

7. Lencioni, *The Five Dysfunctions*.

ministry may result in a greater level of participation in those ministries. Times during worship services when people are given an opportunity to share how God has been using them in mission to others might be a great encouragement to other members to find a way to utilize their gifts and talents to further the work of the Kingdom.

Fifth, love widely. The behavior that scored the lowest on the Congregational Trust Survey and, therefore, was the behavior generating the most mistrust within the studied congregations, was the forming of cliques. Pastors and church leaders face a difficult task in balancing the need of people for close friendships with the biblical mandate to reach out to others. The church must encourage the widening of the circles of friendship to build relationships that exclude no one and welcome everyone. Pastors could model this in their own contacts and relationships within the church. Much of a pastor's time is spent with those within the church who are actively engaged in ministry and there could be the perception that the pastor's "favorites" are those who do the most work or contribute the most financially. When the congregation sees that the pastor does not play favorites within the church but is concerned about every member, regardless of personality, ministry involvement, or financial contribution, it can go a long way in encouraging others to widen their circles of relationships.

Sixth, share information freely. It is essential that congregational members understand that the "goal of decision making in the church is not simply to discover the will of the community, but instead to discern together the will of God."[8] When this concept is clearly understood, people are less likely to play politics within the church to push their own agendas promoting their self-interests. People feel included in the decision-making process when their leaders provide clear information concerning decisions that are being discussed and the reasons confirming that this is the will of God for the congregation. Members want to have adequate information to understand the direction where they are being led.[9] Leaders who provide adequate information are perceived as more trustworthy than those who do not.[10] Pastors must not withhold information that is needed to move the congregation in a common direction because those actions create the perception that pastors have hidden agendas.

---

8. Guder, *Missional Church*, 172.
9. Kouzes and Posner, *Leadership Challenge*.
10. Wanberg and Banas, "Predictors and Outcomes."

Seventh, ask questions. When decisions need to be made regarding changes in the church, pastors need to involve the people most affected by those decisions. Allowing people to provide input and assuring them that their opinions have been heard, understood, and taken seriously, fosters trust within the congregation. Clearly and accurately expressing the views of others helps to prove that they have been understood, which also builds trust. Some pastors may be tempted to utilize manipulative tactics to get people moving in the direction they want their members to go, but manipulation will breed serious mistrust within the congregation. Pastors must realize that they are servants of the church and must never think of people merely as means to further one's agenda.

Eighth, act humbly. The attitudes that are ingrained in people's hearts through living in a "me first" generation and in a culture that promotes self-benefits over corporate needs must be overcome in congregational relationships. As followers of Christ, pastors must seek to emulate the Lord of the Church who did not come to be served but to serve. The human tendency is to seek one's own benefit and to advance one's own interests at the expense of others. The attitude that I must win and others must lose must have no place in the hearts of followers of Christ. Instead, every decision that is made and every action that is taken should put the needs of others before one's own.

Ninth, protect passionately. The results of the Trust Survey showed that not many of the people in the churches studied were trying to get even with each other. This was gratifying to see, considering how such behaviors, far too prevalent in some churches, are in contradiction to the love of God. Jesus admonished his disciples to "do good to those who hurt you, bless those who curse you, pray for those who mistreat you" (Luke 6:27–28), and the Apostle Paul similarly exhorted us to "be kind and compassionate to one another, forgiving each other, just as in Christ God forgave you" (Eph. 4:32). Pastors need to zealously guard their flocks from those who would openly attack others and who would seek revenge for offenses against them. These behaviors are completely contrary to the spirit of Christ and have no place within the Church of Christ.

Tenth, forgive freely. Offenses will happen within churches, and people will be hurt by the wrong actions of others, but the response to those offenses must be forgiveness and a willingness to be reconciled. When those who have been offended extend grace and forgiveness to the offenders, and when offenders repent of their offenses and seek reconciliation, it helps build a climate of trust within the church. Churches must become the communities of reconciliation that God intends for them to be. This vision of the reconciled community, of course, does not mitigate against necessary cautions regarding those whose behavior has demonstrated that they are unsafe for such community. Much of the challenge of practicing authenticity and grace in the body of Christ is that we do so with broken people who live in a broken world. Much wisdom is needed in cases where real harm has been or could be done.

A CALL FOR REPENTANCE

The project unearthed some serious issues that need to be addressed by pastors and denominational leaders. The review of the literature clearly showed how the behaviors tracked by the Trust Survey are violations of biblical commands and ethical principles that are contradictory to the Spirit of Christ. The prevalence of these behaviors in congregations brings disgrace and harm to the Body of Christ. The behaviors are not merely unpleasant aspects of some church cultures but are sins for which people need to repent. The behaviors damage relationships within the fellowship of the church and are actions for which people need to seek reconciliation and forgiveness. Such actions are often tolerated and unaddressed within even the leadership teams of churches, harming local congregations and damaging their reputations in their communities. Pastors should take the lead in repentance and model a contrite and repentant spirit to the congregation when they recognize how their own actions have contributed to an atmosphere of mistrust. James advised the people of God to confess their faults to one another and pray for each other in order for healing to take place. It is evident that spiritual and emotional healing is needed in many American congregations. Congregational members can no longer stand behind the excuses that "This is how I am" and "I will always be this way" and "I will never change." If churches are to break free of their stagnation and move into a season of growth and fruitfulness, confession of sin and repentance will be essential.

Christ intended for his Church to be salt and light in this world, preserving the world from corruption and proclaiming to the world the Gospel. When corruption is at work within the local congregation, eating away at the core of its character, the church cannot be the preserving influence Jesus intended it to be. When relationships within the church are left to fester in disappointment, bitterness, and anger and people refuse to be reconciled with each other, the message the world receives is not Good News but a confirmation of what many suspect: that the church is filled with hypocrites who do not practice what they preach. If revival is to come to Christ's Church, repentance of sin and reconciliation with brothers and sisters must be quickly pursued with a passion.

There are so many factors impacting levels of trust within a congregation that may make it nearly impossible to find common indicators of readiness for or resistance to change. Every congregation is a unique organism, specially equipped and resourced by God to reach its cultural context. Every congregation has a history behind it and a way of working together that is solidified over time. Pastors wanting to implement change may be stymied by the degree to which resistance has been ingrained into the psyche of members. The ability of a church to change may be limited by its history and the degree to which its values and norms are embedded into the consciousness of the members and leaders. The cultural context may have a big part to play as well. As in the case of Church 7981, the mindset of the community may be suspicious of "outsiders," which puts new pastors at a disadvantage. Five to ten years of waiting to be accepted and trusted by a community and congregation could be longer than most pastors are willing to tolerate when they see opportunities missed to reach the lost.

Pastors find themselves at a place in their ministries where they recognize more and more their total dependence upon the Spirit to transform the minds and hearts of church members. It is not for pastors to develop new instruments to manipulate church people to begin doing what they should be doing for God. The Spirit can create within the hearts of God's people a yearning to break free of the chains that have bound them too long in comfortable routines and sleepy rituals. The Spirit can empower those who have merely occupied pews and enable them to incarnate the Gospel in their local contexts. The Spirit is able to create a deep hunger in the hearts of church members to see the lost brought to faith in Christ. The Spirit is able to help God's people to unlearn the old habits of living and to transform their lives into the likeness of Christ, both in his character and in his mission. The Spirit is able to convince God's people of the needs of people around them without Christ and to fill them with confidence in the Spirit's ability to use them to make a positive impact in the lives of co-workers, neighbors, and friends.

God is calling all of his people to enter into the adventure of being part of what he is doing in this world, and this will require full surrender, total dedication, personal change, and a deepened spiritual intimacy in the lives of individual believers. The needs of people without Christ tear at the hearts of those with a Kingdom mindset. When they yield themselves fully to God, he is able to do awesome things in and through their lives. The work that is accomplished through fully-devoted followers of Christ is multiplied when they have covenanted to work together for the sake of a common mission and are fully committed to do whatever needs to be done and to change whatever needs to be changed to fulfill that mission.

WHAT YOU CAN DO NOW

If you describe yourself as a frustrated leader of a not-yet-missional congregation, we hope that you see the encouragement with which we conclude this book. Let's introduce or summarize that encouragement here:

First, while as a leader you have a certain amount of responsibility for the spiritual health of your congregation, your church ultimately belongs to and is under the care of the Holy Spirit. It is not yours; it is his. He called it into existence and he will nurture it, doubtless through your good service (and other means). But, contrary to some of the leadership literature you may have read, not everything "rises and falls on leadership." Remember that Jesus himself was not "successful" in the sense of motivating all or even most of his followers to pursue his mission; he experienced abandonment, frustration, and outright opposition, particularly as he led his disciples into the deeper things of God. And he is the one who continually encourages us to "fear not." We serve as stewards, for a while, of a congregation of God's people, and as we trust him to do his work among them, the burden on our shoulders eases, and his grace flows. Trust him.

Second, your own behavior does have an impact on the health of your congregation, but it's probably less in the agenda and vision you pursue and more in the kind of relationships you establish. The behaviors described earlier in this chapter that build trust—these are also indicators of a mature believer in Christ. And these come almost always through pain. Whether the pain is personal in nature or professional (such as the frustrations of attempting to lead people where they are not inclined to go), the molding of character that the Spirit invites in such experiences can soften our hearts, make gentle our spirit, and build true authenticity and grace in our relationships. And just when we think we have failed to move people forward, we may find that in the creation of relationships of trust, we are granted more authority or respect than we would ever have earned through mere organizational effectiveness. Sometimes we must fail before we can succeed. Maybe no one should be fully trusted as a leader until she or he has experienced a significant failure or loss, for it is those breaking experiences that best prepare us to exercise power or authority with grace.

Third, there are tools by which you can help your congregation to see itself, as in a mirror. Many maintenance-type churches actually have a positive self-image. They think they are loving because they love each other (but not the newcomer). They think they are evangelistic because they remember having been converted. They think they are following Jesus because they worship and serve faithfully. But a tool like the Congregational Trust Survey (or a number of other fine instruments out there) can reveal patterns of behavior and attitude that are known but seldom acknowledged. Such revelations can be disturbing, of course, and pushback may follow, as we have illustrated in this volume. But they can also be opportunities for self-examination, perhaps even repentance and renewal. Walk into such opportunities with prayer and discernment, but, again, fear not. God often shows up most obviously in moments when our masks are dropped and we see ourselves as we really are.

Fourth, you can name and question some of your own assumptions about what it means to be "missional." Our culture has been addicted to "bigger, better, and faster" for so long now that American churches and their leaders often naturally assume that church health or spiritual maturity necessarily entails a growth in metrics. Leonard Sweet refers to these as the ABCs: attendance, buildings, and cash.[11] This has been the foundation of the church growth movement and the megachurch model. But it is increasingly apparent that these are not the New Testament indicators of effective leadership. When Paul encourages the Ephesians to a greater love for each other, to maturity in how they exercise their spiritual gifts, to reconciliation across cultural and other barriers, and to standing firm in their faith, he is advocating something far richer and, yes, more "missional" than what many American church leaders aspire to. So perhaps Sweet's description of the Church as "so beautiful" may capture the essence of the biblical vision of congregational life more than any metric can.

---

11. Leonard Sweet, *So Beautiful*.

Fifth, you can pray. And we can and will join you in that prayer, for we believe that this prayer speaks something close to the heart of God for his Church. So may God graciously grant to the churches of North America, including yours and ours, a fresh wave of his Spirit, transforming local congregations with a new sense of mission. May her leaders, including you and us, recommit themselves to wholeheartedly modeling the behaviors that build trust, so that, reaching out together with all of God's people, they might win new lovers of Jesus and guide older ones to love him even more. May her local congregations, including yours and ours, rejoice in all the good accomplished through the traditions of the past, but may they be willing to lay aside those traditions for new ministries that are faithful in speaking to the needs of their unique communities. And may God's will be done on earth, including in our own lives, as it is done in heaven. Amen.

Appendix A

Congregational Trust Survey

Please rank each of the following statements according to what you have personally observed in your church:

The people in our congregation: Almost Never ↔ Almost Always

1. Say one thing but do another.	4	3	2	1	0
2. Make agreements they do not keep.	4	3	2	1	0
3. Say one thing to one person and something else to another person.	4	3	2	1	0
4. Pretend to agree with others.	4	3	2	1	0
5. Try to discredit others.	4	3	2	1	0
6. Focus on others' mistakes.	4	3	2	1	0
7. Withhold information.	4	3	2	1	0
8. Make excuses for mistakes.	4	3	2	1	0
9. Undercut others.	4	3	2	1	0
10. Gossip about others.	4	3	2	1	0
11. Play politics to get what they want.	4	3	2	1	0
12. Form themselves into cliques.	4	3	2	1	0
13. Seek win-lose outcomes.	4	3	2	1	0
14. Look out for their own interests.	4	3	2	1	0
15. Use manipulative tactics.	4	3	2	1	0
16. Make decisions affecting others without involving others.	4	3	2	1	0
17. Put each other down.	4	3	2	1	0

Appendix A

18. Blame others for mistakes.	4	3	2	1	0
19. Have hidden agendas.	4	3	2	1	0
20. Compete with each other.	4	3	2	1	0
21. Try to get even with each other.	4	3	2	1	0
22. Criticize each other.	4	3	2	1	0
23. Have a "we-they" mentality.	4	3	2	1	0
24. Openly attack each other.	4	3	2	1	0
25. Give more negative feedback than positive.	4	3	2	1	0
26. Spring surprises on each other.	4	3	2	1	0
27. Ignore input from others.	4	3	2	1	0
28. Try to intimidate each other.	4	3	2	1	0
29. Use information to their own advantage.	4	3	2	1	0
30. Distort what other people say.	4	3	2	1	0

Adapted from Ken Hultman, *Making Change Irresistible: Overcoming Resistance to Change in your Organization*. (Palo Alto, CA: Davies-Black, 1998), 164.

Appendix B

Pastors' Follow-up Survey

OVER THE PAST YEAR, have you attempted to implement any kind of missional change within the congregation or community where you are serving? If so, would you please briefly share the kind of change and what you were hoping to accomplish through this?

On a scale of 1 to 5, how much resistance or willingness did you encounter to the proposed change?

1–Very Resistant
2–Some Resistance
3–Neutral
4–Somewhat Willing
5–Very Willing

What kinds of resistance did you encounter to the proposal? Check all that pertain.

___ Verbal attack

___ Appeal to reason

___ Emotional withdrawal

___ Left the church

___ Attack on motives

___ Feet-dragging

___ Blank stares

Appendix B

___ Withdrew financial support of the church

___ Used the Bible as proof why such a change should not be considered

___ Spiritual warfare

___ "We don't have enough information to be able to make such a decision"

___ "That was not how the Church in Acts did things."

___ "We don't have enough money to be able to support such an idea."

___ "We tried that before and it did not work."

___ "We've never done that before."

___ "This is just how we are, and we are never going to change."

___ "We don't know if this is going to work."

___ "We are going to lose our power and control in the congregation."

___ "I have served in this position all these years, and are you telling me now that everything I have done was of no lasting value?"

___ "We have gone through too many changes in recent years, and we can't take anymore."

___ "I don't see how this change is going to benefit me or my family."

___ "The problem with these preachers is that they are always ramming change down our throats; always trying to boss us around."

___ "I like my church the way that it is, and I don't want it to change."

___ "I am not really convinced that the pastor has our best interests at heart."

___ "Our congregational leaders don't really listen to what we are saying or understand how we are feeling."

If you have any additional comments about congregational resistance to change, please include them here.

If you have any additional comments about the Congregational Trust Survey, please include them here.

Thanks so much for your assistance in completing this project!

Bibliography

Anderson, Jon. "The Weight of History: An Exploration of Resistance to Change in Vicars/ Managers." *Creativity and Innovation Management* 9, no. 3 (Sep 2000): 147–155. *Business Source Premier*, EBSCO*host*, (accessed 3 November 2005) (AN: 5384634).

Anderson, Leith. *Leadership that Works: Hope and Direction for Church and Parachurch Leaders in Today's Complex World*. Minneapolis: Bethany House, 1999.

Anderson, Linda Ackerman and Dean Anderson. "How to Build a Critical Mass of Support to Accelerate your Change." *Results from Change* 13 (December 2002) www .being first.com/results from change.

Bauckham, Richard J. *Jude, 2 Peter*. Vol. 50 of *Word Biblical Commentary*. Edited by Ralph P. Martin. Waco: Word, 1983.

Beitler, Michael. *Strategic Organizational Change: Second Edition*. Greensboro: Practitioner, 2006.

Bishop, Charles H. *Making Change Happen One Person at a Time: Assessing Change Capacity within your Organization*. New York: AMACOM, 2000.

Blackaby, Henry and Claude King. *Experiencing God: How to Live the Full Adventure of Knowing and Doing the Will of God*. Nashville: Broadman and Holman, 1994.

Blair, Anthony. "Revivalism and Democratization: The Church of the United Brethren in Christ before the Civil War." *Journal of United Brethren History and Life* 1, no. 1 (2000): 27–46.

Bridges, William. *Managing Transitions: Making the Most of Change*. Reading, MA: Addison-Wesley, 1991.

Bridges, William and Susan Mitchell. (2000). Leading Transitions: A New Model for Change. *Leader to Leader* 16 (Spring 2000): 30–36. www.pfdf.org/leaderbooks (accessed 27 February 2006).

Burke, H. Dale. "Even Healthy Churches Need to Change," *Leadership Journal*, 1 October 2005, http://www.christianitytoday.com/le/2005/fall/3.43.html (13 December 2005).

Burke, Spencer and Colleen Pepper. (2003). *Making Sense of Church: Eavesdropping on Emerging Conversations about God, Community and Culture*. Grand Rapids: Zondervan, 2003.

Cadbury, Henry Joel. "Gospel Study and our Image of Early Christianity." *Journal of Biblical Literature* 83, no.2 (1 June 1964): 139–145. ATLA Religion Database with ATLA Serials, EBSCO*host* (accessed 24 October 2006). (AN: ATLA0000688185).

Caughlin, Jerrold J. "Emotional Factors Producing Resistance to Change." *Pastoral Psychology* (March 1972): 23–28.

Charnock, Stephen. *Discourses upon the Existence and Attributes of God*. Grand Rapids: Baker, 1979.

Bibliography

Chase, Michael. "Covert Processes in Corporate Church Life: A Tavistock Perspective." (1990). www.mikechaseleadership.com/WebTAV190_APA.htm (accessed 13 February 2007).

Clines, David J. A. *Ezra, Nehemiah, Esther. The New Century Bible Commentary.* Edited by R. E. Clements. Grand Rapids: Eerdmans, 1984.

Cloud, Henry. *Integrity: The Courage to Meet the Demands of Reality.* New York: Harper Collins, 2006.

Cohen, Dan S. *The Heart of Change Field Guide: Tools and Tactics for Leading Change in your Organization.* Boston: Harvard Business School, 2005.

Cooperrider, David L. and Diana Whitney. *Appreciative Inquiry: A Positive Revolution in Change.* San Francisco: Berrett-Koehler, 2005.

Cornelius, Ed. "Leading a Culture Ready for Change." *Executive Excellence*, 20, no. 7 (July 2003): 15. *Business Source Premier*, EBSCO*host* (accessed 7 November 2012). (AN: 10539127).

Covey, Stephen M. R. *The Speed of Trust: The One Thing that Changes Everything.* New York: Free Press, 2006.

Demarest, Gary W. *1, 2 Thessalonians, 1, 2 Timothy, Titus.* Vol. 9 of *The Communicator's Commentary.* Edited by Lloyd J. Ogilvie. Waco: Word, 1984.

Ehrlich, Howard J. and Dorothy Lee. "Dogmatism, Learning, and Resistance to Change: A Review and a New Paradigm." *Psychological Bulletin* 71, no. 4 (April 1969): 249–260. *PsycARTICLES*, EBSCO*host* (accessed 30 October 2012). (AN: 1969-08253-001).

Escobar, Samuel. *The New Global Mission: The Gospel from Everywhere to Everyone.* Downers Grove: InterVarsity, 2003.

Ferrin, Donald L., Kurt T. Dirks, and Pri P. Shah. "Direct and Indirect Effects of Third-party Relationships on Interpersonal Trust." *Journal of Applied Psychology* 91, no. 4 (July 2006): 870–883. *PsycARTICLES*, EBSCO*host* (accessed October 30, 2012). (AN: 2006-08435-01).

Frost, Michael. *Exiles: Living Missionally in a Post-Christian Culture.* Peabody, MA: Hendrickson, 2006.

Fullan, Michael, Claudia Cuttress, and Ann Kilcher. "Eight Forces for Leaders of Change: Presence of the Core Concepts Does Not Guarantee Success, but Their Absence Ensures Failure." *Journal Of Staff Development* 26, no. 4 (January 1, 2005): 54–58. *ERIC*, EBSCO*host* (accessed October 30, 2012).

Gardner, Howard. *Changing Minds: The Art and Science of Changing our Own and Other People's Minds.* Boston: Harvard Business School, 2004.

Goleman, Daniel. *Emotional Intelligence.* New York: Bantam Dell, 2006.

Guder, Darrell L., ed. *Missional Church: A Vision for the Sending of the Church in North America.* Grand Rapids: Eerdmans, 1998.

Henderson, Mark. "Battle-scarred Reflections: Lessons Learned from the Front Lines of Organizational Transformation." (2000). www.managerwise.com (accessed 29 December 2005).

Hiatt, Jeff. *ADKAR: A Model for Change in Business, Government and our Community: How to Implement Successful Change in our Personal Lives and Professional Careers.* Loveland, CO: Prosci Research, 2006.

Hinds, Manuel. *The Triumph of the Flexible Society: The Connectivity Revolution and Resistance to Change.* Westport, CT: Praeger, 2003.

Bibliography

Hulshizer, Steve. "Marks of a New Testament Church: How should a New Testament Church Function?" *Christian News and Views,* 10 December 2005, www.cnview.com/churches_today/marks_of_a_new_testament_church.htm

Hultman, Ken. *Making Change Irresistible: Overcoming Resistance to Change in your Organization.* Palo Alto: Davies-Black, 1998.

Hultman, Ken and Bill Gellerman. *Balancing Individual and Organizational Values: Walking the Tightrope to Success.* San Francisco: Jossey-Bass/Pfeiffer, 2002.

Izard, Carroll E. "Personality Characteristics Associated with Resistance to Change." *Journal of Consulting Psychology* 24, no. 5 (October 1960): 437–440. PsycARTICLES EBSCO*host* (accessed 30 October 2012) (AN: 1961-04985-001).

Jellison, Jerald M. *Overcoming Resistance: A Practical Guide for Producing Change in the Workplace.* New York: Simon & Schuster, 1993.

Kane, J. Herbert. *Understanding Christian Missions.* Grand Rapids: Baker, 1978.

Kanter, Rosabeth Moss. "The Enduring Skills of Change Leaders." *Leader to Leader Institute* 13, (Summer 1999): 15–22. www.pfdf.org/leaderbooks (accessed 12 December 2005).

Kegan, Robert, and Lisa Laskow Lahey,. *Immunity to Change: How to Overcome it and Unlock the Potential in Yourself and Your Organization.* Boston: Harvard Business School, 2009.

Kerber, Kenneth and Anthony F. Buono. "Rethinking Organizational Change: Reframing the Challenge of Change Management." *Organization Development Journal* 23, no. 3 (Fall 2005): 23–38. Business Source Premier, EBSCO*host* (accessed 30 October 2012) (AN: 19282862)

Kimball, Dan. *The Emerging Church: Vintage Christianity for New Generations.* Grand Rapids: Zondervan, 2003.

Kotter, John P. *A Sense of Urgency.* Boston: Harvard Business School, 2008.

Kotter, John P. *Leading Change.* Boston: Harvard Business School, 1996.

Kotter, John P., and Dan S. Cohen. *The Heart of Change: Real-life Stories of How Individuals Changed their Organizations.* Boston: Harvard Business School, 2002.

Kouzes, James M. and Barry Z. Posner. *The Leadership Challenge: Third Edition.* San Francisco: Jossey-Bass, 2002.

Kouzes, James M. and Barry Z. Posner. "Challenge is the Opportunity for Greatness." *Leader to Leader* 28, 2003. www.pfdf.org/leaderbooks (accessed 25 May 2006).

Latting, Jean Kantanbu, and V. Jean Ramsey. *Reframing Change: How to Deal with Workplace Dynamics, Influence Others, and Bring People Together to Initiate Positive Change.* Santa Barbara: ABC-CLIO, 2009.

Lawrence, Paul R. "How to Deal with Resistance to Change." *Harvard Business Review* (January-February 1969).

Lencioni, Patrick. *The Five Dysfunctions of a Team: A Leadership Fable.* San Francisco: Jossey-Bass, 2002.

Lewis, Robert and Wayne Cordeiro. *Culture Shift: Transforming your Church from the Inside Out.* San Francisco: Jossey-Bass, 2005.

Lines, Rune, Marcus Selart, Bjarne Espedal, and Svein Johansen. "The Production of Trust during Organizational Change." *Journal of Change Management* 5 (June 2005): 221–245. Business Source Premier, EBSCO*host* (accessed 6 November 2012). (AN: 10.1080/14697010500143555).

Loup, Roland, and Ron Koller. "The Road to Commitment: Capturing the Head, Hearts and Hands of People to Effect Change." *Organization Development Journal* 23, no. 3

Bibliography

(Fall 2005): 73–81. *Business Source Premier*, EBSCO*host* (accessed 7 October 2005) (AN: 19282866).

Marshak, Robert J. "Morphing: The Leading Edge of Organizational Change in the Twenty-first Century." *Organizational Development Journal*, 22, no. 3 (Fall 2004): 8–21. *Business Source Premier*, EBSCO*host* (accessed October 7, 2005). (AN: 15592313).

Maurer, Rick. (2001). *Why Resistance Matters*. www.refresher.com/!resistancematters.html (accessed 29 November 2005).

Maxwell, John. *The 21 Irrefutable Laws of Leadership*. Nashville: Thomas Nelson, 1998.

McLaren, Brian. *The Church on the Other Side: Doing Ministry in the Postmodern Matrix*. Grand Rapids: Zondervan, 2000.

McManus, Erwin Raphael. *An Unstoppable Force: Daring to Become the Church God had in Mind*. Loveland, CO: Flagship Church Resources. 2001.

McNeal, Reggie. *Revolution in Leadership: Training Apostles for Tomorrow's Church*. Nashville: Abingdon, 1998.

Minatrea, Milfred. *Shaped by God's Heart: The Passion and Practices of Missional Churches*. San Francisco: Jossey-Bass, 2004.

O'Toole, James. *Leading Change: Overcoming the Ideology of Comfort and the Tyranny of Custom*. San Francisco: Jossey-Bass, 1995.

Olsen, Ted. "'I am guilty of sexual immorality... a deceiver and a liar,' Haggard confesses." *Christianity Today*, (5 November 2006). www.christianitytoday.com/ct/2006/novemberweb-only/144-58.0.html

Oreg, Shaul. "Resistance to Change: Developing an Individual Differences Measure." *Journal of Applied Psychology* 88, no. 4 (August 2003): 680-693. *Business Source Premier*, EBSCO*host* (accessed November 7, 2012).

Palmer, Brien. *Making Change Work: Practical Tools for Overcoming Human Resistance to Change*. Milwaukee: Quality Press, 2003.

Rafferty, Alannah E. and Mark A. Griffin. "Perceptions of Organizational Change: A Stress and Coping Perspective." *Journal of Applied Psychology* 91, no. 5 (September 2006): 1154–1162. *PsycARTICLES* EBSCO*host* (accessed 30 October 2012). (AN: 2006-11397-014).

Reale, Richard C. *Making Change Stick: Twelve Principles for Transforming Organizations*. Park Ridge, NJ: Positive Impact Associates, 2005.

Rendle, Gilbert R. *Leading Change in the Congregation: Spiritual and Organizational Tools for Leaders*. Herndon, VA: Alban Institute, 1998.

Rousseau, Denise M. and Snehal A. Tijoriwala. "What's a Good Reason to Change? Motivated Reasoning and Social Accounts in Promoting Organizational Change." *Journal of Applied Psychology* 84, no.4 (August 1999): 514–528. *PsycARTICLES* EBSCO*host* (accessed 26 October 2006) (AN: 1999-11038-004).

Schneider, William E. "Why Good Management Ideas Fail—The Neglected Power of Organizational Culture." *Focus on Change Management* (May-June, 1998). www.refresher.com (accessed 27 February 2006).

Senge, Peter, C. Otto Scharmer, Joseph Jaworski and Betty Sue Flowers. *Presence: An Exploration of Profound Change in People, Organizations and Society*. Westminster, MD: Bantam-Dell, 2005.

Sweet, Leonard. *soulTsunami: Sink or Swim in New Millennium Culture*. Grand Rapids: Zondervan, 1999

Bibliography

Van Gelder, Craig. "From Corporate Church to Missional Church: The Challenge Facing Congregations Today." *Review and Expositor* 101, no. 3 (Summer 2004): 425–450. (ATLA database)

Wanberg, Connie. & Banas, Joseph T. (2000). "Predictors and Outcomes of Openness to Changes in a Reorganizing Workplace." *Journal of Applied Psychology* 85, no. 1 (Feb. 2000): 132–142. PsycArticles, EBSCO*host*. (accessed 26 October 2006), (AN: 2000-03754-014).

Wesley, John. *Commentary on 1 Peter 5: John Wesley's Explanatory Notes,* 1765. www.studylight.org/com/wen/view.cgi?book=1pe&chapter=005 (accessed 1 January 2007).

Winter, Ralph D. and Bruce A. Koch. "Finishing the Task: The Unreached Peoples Challenge," *U. S. Center for World Mission*, 16 December 2006, www.uscwm.org/uploads/pdf/psp/winter_koch_finishingthetask.pdf

www.ingramcontent.com/pod-product-compliance
Lightning Source LLC
Chambersburg PA
CBHW071502160426
43195CB00013B/2186